Please Listen ...

Please Listen ...

Queenship Publishing Company
P. O. Box 42028
Santa Barbara, California 93140-2028
Phone (800) 647-9882 Fax (805) 569-3274

According to a decree of the Congregation for the Doctrine of Faith, approved by H.H. Pope Paul VI, (1966), it is permitted to publish, without an imprimatur, texts relating to new revelations, apparitions, prophecies or miracles.

The Publisher recognizes and accepts that the final authority regarding the messages at Scottsdale, Arizona rests with the Holy See of Rome, to whose judgment we willingly submit.

- The Publisher

Cover Credits:
Front cover: Interior photograph of St. Maria Goretti Catholic Church, Scottsdale, Arizona by Deacon Len Zbiegien.

Back cover: Exterior photograph of St. Maria Goretti Catholic Church, Scottsdale, Arizona by Roger Baele.

Published By Queenship Publishing Company
P.O. Box 42028
Santa Barbara, CA 93140-2028
Phone (800) 647-9882 Fax (800) 569-3274

Printed in the United States of America

Library of Congress Catalog # 94-69790

ISBN: 1-882972-52-X

INTRODUCTION

This book is a compilation of all the messages from Jesus Christ and His mother, The Blessed Virgin Mary, received during "Our Lady's Prayer Group" at St. Maria Goretti Roman Catholic Church in Scottsdale, Arizona. The book begins with the first recorded message of July 14, 1988 and ends with August 18th, 1994, though the messages continue.

The Thursday evening prayer group has formed after a parish pilgrimage by over 100 people to Medujorge in the fall of 1987. It was created in response to Our Lady's call to join together in prayer, to focus on her Son, Jesus Christ, His gospel message, the faith as taught by His church, and to place God in the center of their lives.

In July of 1988, Our Lady first, and then Our Lord, began visiting the prayer group with messages of encouragement, love and peace, inviting everyone to accept His mercy and healing. The locutions from Our Lady have been given through three young adults , principally Gianna (Talone) Sullivan. At times, Our Lord has spoken through pastor, Fr. Jack Spaulding, after the gospel of Thursday Night's mass.

The prayer group is open to all; it begins every Thursday evening at 7:00 pm in the church beginning with the praying of the joyful mysteries of the rosary, followed by the Chaplet of Divine Mercy, celebrating of the mass, praying the glorious mysteries, blessing of religious articles, and ending with a prayer of healing.

Designed as a simple study-guide, this book is meant not only to be read as a series of messages, but also to be reflected upon. It is hoped that the readers will be able to apply these messages to their daily lives, and to find them helpful in their personal journey to holiness.

It is not the purpose of this book to explain the events occurring in Scottsdale. Several books have been written about the events at St. Maria Goretti Parish by noted theologians and mariologists. For a list of publications and a recently produced documentary, please refer to page 106 in the back of this book.

JULY 14, 1988
MESSAGE FROM OUR LADY

My children, open your hearts to Jesus. He wants to fill you with His grace. He wants to give you His joy and He wants your joy to be complete. Pray, pray, pray! Know that Jesus is real! Accept your suffering so that Jesus can heal you. Give glory and praise to my Son, Jesus!

Notes & Reflections:

JULY 21, 1988
MESSAGE FROM OUR LADY

My children, why are you so reluctant to open your hearts? What does it take to convince you? Why is it you must see to believe? I tell you, look within and you shall see.

My children, without Jesus you can achieve nothing. Please place Jesus at the center of your lives. I invite you to allow Jesus to make you beautiful. With Jesus you can achieve everything.

Notes & Reflections:

JULY 28, 1988
MESSAGE FROM OUR LADY

My children, you know that all you need do is walk in God's way and heed His commandments and you will prosper, but yet you cannot and you wonder why. It is because you will not abandon yourself to Jesus. You want to control. If you allow Jesus to be the center of your lives and accept what He brings, He will bless you and all your work, and you will prosper.

Notes & Reflections:

AUGUST 5, 1988
MESSAGE FROM OUR LADY

My dear children, if only you knew how beautiful you are when you pray. Much glory is given to Jesus when your prayer is from your heart. Thank you, my dear children.

Notes & Reflections:

AUGUST 5, 1988
MESSAGE FROM OUR LADY

My dear children, on this day nothing would please me more than for you to seek the kingdom of God. Please pray. You are so beautiful, my dear children, when you pray. It is my wish to teach you and that you be with Jesus in heaven. It will not be difficult. Simply focus on Jesus in all your pleasures and trials, and glory will be given to Him.

Be happy, my little ones. Jesus will deliver you from your turmoil and guide you. You need only to love, pray with your heart, be humble and keep Jesus at the very center of your life. Thank you, my dear children.

Notes & Reflections:

AUGUST 11, 1988
MESSAGE FROM OUR LADY

My dear children, it is my wish to help save you and for you to be with me in Heaven. Only Jesus can save you. Please pray! You believe and then you don't believe. You must fully believe to enter the Kingdom of God. Please convert. Do not pray with your lips but with your heart.

I tell you, Jesus sees everything you do and has great love for you. Please be on your best behavior. Thank you, my dear loved ones.

Notes & Reflections:

AUGUST 18, 1988
MESSAGE FROM OUR LADY

Oh my children, I cry because there are so many of my children who do not want to be with Jesus in Heaven. I want everybody to be happy and to be with Jesus in Heaven. Please consecrate yourself to Jesus. We invite you to total happiness.

Notes & Reflections:

AUGUST 25, 1988
MESSAGE FROM OUR LADY

My children, Jesus accepted His crown of thorns with love and died for the forgiveness of your sins, so that you would be able to be with Him in Heaven filled with His joy. It is important to begin loving one another, so that you will be filled with this special joy of Jesus. You will experience happiness by loving one another, because Jesus lives in everyone, and by loving one another, you love Jesus, and His treasures will be given to you. Thank you, my loved ones, and peace to you.

Notes & Reflections:

SEPTEMBER 1, 1988
MESSAGE FROM OUR LADY

Oh my children, soon you will be filled with so much joy. Please pray. Pray as you have not prayed before, with all your strength, with all your heart. Pray so that I will be able to take your prayers and answer them. Bless you, my dear children, and rejoice in the living God!
Notes & Reflections:

SEPTEMBER 8, 1988
MESSAGE FROM OUR LADY

My dear children, do not be afraid. Jesus, Who is living, is your shield.
Notes & Reflections:

SEPTEMBER 15, 1988
MESSAGE FROM OUR LADY

My dear children, thank you for responding to the light; the light of eternal life. Oh my dear children, you are so beautiful; beautiful like a growing flower, and Jesus is your vine.
Notes & Reflections:

SEPTEMBER 15, 1988
MESSAGE FROM OUR LADY

My dear children, in today's world there are so many unbelievers. People rely on their own knowledge which they think is their source of greatness. They forget where that knowledge comes from. It brings me great pain to see children, my children, who must have proof to believe. It is like buying love. This cannot be, for love is a deep passion which flows with purity. It is through this love, purity and quiet dignity, that Jesus conquers.

Please pray for unbelievers; the people who cannot be happy or peaceful because they will not surrender themselves to Jesus, the people who must see to believe, the people who will not go beyond the prayer of speaking words, instead of the prayer which should be from their heart. I invite you again, this day, my dear children, to let God dwell in the deepest, most center of your life. Jesus, Who is your source of strength, energy and fresh wholeness, awaits your love.
Notes & Reflections:

SEPTEMBER 22 1988
MESSAGE FROM OUR LADY

My dear children, please trust in Jesus. Totally surrender all your thoughts and actions to Jesus and be at peace by letting Him provide for you. Jesus will never harm you and will fill you with what you need; for to trust Jesus is to love Jesus.
Notes & Reflections:

SEPTEMBER 29, 1988
MESSAGE FROM OUR LADY

My dear children, it is my wish for you to be happy. True happiness comes from surrendering yourself to Jesus, by opening your hearts to His words. If you will allow Jesus to be at the center of your life and dwell on Him, all your problems will be minor. Dwell on Jesus, not your problems. Pray for the Holy Spirit to guide you and lead you in all your actions.

I know you are tired, my children, but I your mother am tireless and wish to comfort you. Surrender to me and trust. I will present you to Jesus in a way which is pleasing to Him. Thank you, my dear ones, for responding to my call.
Notes & Reflections:

OCTOBER 6, 1988
MESSAGE FROM OUR LADY

Oh my children, with surrendering there is so much comfort. Jesus is not asking you to be any different than the person you are. He wants you to experience the beauty of simplicity. He is simply calling you to happiness by loving. Allow your love to be shared by passing it on through your words, actions and deeds. Love is the simplest, most beautiful and purest form of prayer. Jesus does not want any of you to suffer. He suffered for you. He wants you to be filled with His love and for you to live it.

Ask, my children, and you will receive. Ask with purity and simplicity. Trust like a child trusts that he will be cared for. Seek the truth and the truth will lead you to eternal life. Knock and the Holy Spirit shall be given to you to sanctify you in His holiness. It is very simple - love as you want to be loved. Live with peace and share His happiness and eternal life. Thank you, my children, for responding to my call.
Notes & Reflections:

OCTOBER 13, 1988
MESSAGE FROM OUR LADY

My dear children, please begin loving one another. It is necessary that you begin loving your family and parishioners so it will be easier to accept what is to follow. Return to basic principles of loving and respecting one another. Let all your daily activities and work be offered as a form of prayer to Jesus. This glorifies Him and many graces are given. Jesus is alive and He lives in each one of you.

It is time for you to share the love of Jesus with those who are struggling. Pass on your love and reach out to one another. Your reward of peace and happiness will be unmeasurable. Thank you for responding to my call.

Notes & Reflections:

OCTOBER 27, 1988
MESSAGE FROM OUR LADY

My children, I am here because of the love Jesus has for you. Oh my dear ones, won't you please allow Jesus to put His arms around you and comfort you? He simply wants you to live a happy life. He does not want you to be any other person than the special one you are.

Please stop fighting against each other. Join your forces and fight together for God. Put the shield of Jesus on and He will bring you comfort. Thank you, my dear children, for responding to my call.

Notes & Reflections:

NOVEMBER 10, 1988
MESSAGE FROM OUR LADY

My beloved, Jesus is rejected by many. He has been rejected ever since He hung on the cross and is rejected now.

The Kingdom is here, the reign of God is here. It is up to you to beg mercy of my Son... upon you and those whom my Son has sent into your life. In that way you will show Him that you do not reject Him. The time is short; make no mistake about it.

Be serious about your conversion, not gloomy, but serious. If you work an eight hour day then you need to work equally as hard upon your conversion. If you study eight hours a day, you need to work equally as hard on your conversion. If you are retired and have time on your hands, I beg you, don't waste it. Now is the time... think... listen. He is sending you His heart. He is sending me to you... listen, continue to listen. This world is causing Jesus to weep and to continue to be in agony. Pray, have mercy on others, so that my Jesus can have mercy upon you.

Notes & Reflections:

NOVEMBER 17, 1988
MESSAGE FROM OUR LADY

Be at peace, my dear ones, the time for your visitation has come. I love you. You have given your heart to me... I love you for that. I am so overjoyed that you love Jesus, that you have decided to follow Him, that you will try to follow Him more and more every day.

Do not fear anything. The evil one has now been conquered. I will be with you from this day on. Consecrate your heart to Jesus and me. We will be with you so that we can offer your prayers to the Father. Please give me the desire of your heart this night.
Notes & Reflections:

DECEMBER 1, 1988
MESSAGE FROM OUR LADY
(PART ONE)

My dear ones, you pray for peace. What you need to pray for first is obedience and then you will have peace. You need to listen again to the words of my Son. He wishes to grace you with peace but first you need to obey Him. Please obey Him. He wants you to be obedient children. To obey Him you need to listen closely to what He asks. If you listen to His words you will obey Him, and then you will have peace.

Know that He loves you. Know that I love you and I am praying that you will be obedient children to Jesus. With this obedience will come sacrifice, will come trust, will come surrender, and will come abandonment. Obedience is the first gift that you can give to my Jesus.
Notes & Reflections:

DECEMBER 1, 1988
MESSAGE FROM OUR LADY
(PART TWO)

My dear children, my Jesus died for you and He would die again for you because of the love He has for you. Please begin to practice and live the words I speak to you for my Jesus.

Begin by your actions and deeds to live with peace. Do not only pray for peace, live peacefully. This world can be a peaceful one if my children would begin to live with peace. Please try. Let this peace begin with you and it will flow out onto others because they will sense it through your actions. Jesus lives and loves you. Please live His words. Thank you for responding to the call of my Jesus.
Notes & Reflections:

DECEMBER 8, 1988
MESSAGE FROM OUR LADY
(PART ONE)

My dear ones, as you celebrate the feast of my Immaculate Conception, I beg you to allow my Jesus to make you immaculate in your spirit and in your heart. If you give Him your heart, He will be able to clean your heart of all that is not of Him. Do not be afraid any longer. You give so much joy to Jesus and to me in your love. Allow Him to cleanse you of every stain and offer you as a pure gift to God Our Father.

In His goodness He has given me to you. Accept this gift from Him. Come to me, and I will be able to lead you to Jesus. With me it is easier for you to come to Jesus. Make no mistake, there are other ways, but they are much more difficult. He has given me to you so that I can present you to Him.

Please, my dear ones, allow me that gift, to present you to Him. Thank you for listening to me this night with your heart.
Notes & Reflections:

DECEMBER 8, 1988
MESSAGE FROM OUR LADY
(PART TWO)

My dear children, I rejoice today because I, this day, said "yes" to my Jesus as you have said yes. In saying yes to my Jesus, I said yes to serve you. My coming into the world destroyed the sin of Eve. It was I who restored the hope that you would be free of sin.

With your open hearts I can present your sin to Jesus who has conquered sin. Let Him save you. Please, He wants to free you from your turmoil. Come to me. I, pure of heart, shall purify you and present you to Him. He will be the fresh running water which will wash away your sins. Thank you, my dear ones. It is today that I say yes, again, to serve you.
Notes & Reflections:

DECEMBER 15, 1988
MESSAGE FROM OUR LADY

My dear ones, the sorrow in the crucifixion of my Jesus resulted in your joy. It was in His death that you were united to Him. He invites you to receive His grace. He wishes to unite you with Him in His grace. Join your forces and give thanks to my Son, your King! Be glad for the many tidings which are to come.

Pray for His grace! He is extending an invitation to you to receive His grace. There is no sorrow with His grace. There is no pain. There is only comfort and happiness. Pray to Him, my children, and focus on Him as the center of your radiance.
Notes & Reflections:

DECEMBER 15, 1988
MESSAGE FROM OUR LORD

As My Father sent John the Baptist to prepare the people for My coming, so I have sent you My mother to prepare you for My coming. My children, listen to her as she prepares you. Be ready for My grace. Establish within yourself a place for Me, so that when My mother continues to prepare you for My coming, you will have a place in your heart for My presence.

You have opened your heart this much. I tell you I am grateful, but there are many who have not yet opened their hearts. I ask you to pray with My mother, to pray with Me to God, Our Eternal Father, for the salvation of these dear ones that I wish to save. You are blessed! My mother will show you how blessed you are. My words to you are these: "Listen to her, because I listen to her!"

Notes & Reflections:

DECEMBER 22, 1988
MESSAGE FROM OUR LADY

My dear ones, my soul still magnifies the Lord through you... now! I want you to know how happy I am, and how joyful you make me. My heart overflows with tears of joy. As you celebrate my Son's birth, I want you to know how He loves you, and how He would die again and again for you. He gives me to you now! I will be with you now wherever you are. All you need do is go into your heart and I am there. You have already prepared a place for Him... (audible weeping here). He thanks you (in a whisper), and He loves you because you love Him. And I thank you for loving me so much.

You are so dear to me (whispered with great emotion). I am with you! May the peace of my Son, and His ever-present blessing be with you. I love you, my dear ones. You do have His mercy... because you are trying to have mercy on others. Thank you for your obedience.

Notes & Reflections:

DECEMBER 29, 1988
MESSAGE FROM OUR LADY

My dear children, I am your Lady of Joy. I am joyful because of the hope I bring of my Jesus. He is your hope, your joy. And I am here to take you to Him. Please! Pray for peace! This world will change with your prayers. If you do not pray for peace, it is sure not to come.

I rejoice because of you, my children. You have given me your heart. I come to all who give me their heart, and I am now here with you because you have given me your heart. In giving me your heart, my Jesus has given you His heart. There is hope, my children, through your prayers. Thank you.

Notes & Reflections:

DECEMBER 29, 1988
MESSAGE FROM OUR LORD

My children, as My mother and Joseph presented Me to My Father in Heaven, that day of My presentation, I have allowed her to present you to Me. Please allow her to present you to God, Our Father.

Keep My commandments; have mercy on each other. And as you have mercy on each other, I then will have mercy on you. She so much wants to present you to My Father. I have allowed her to do that. I love you with a heart that is open and that has been open since she presented Me to My Father.

When she presented Me to My Father, My Father gave Me back... not only to her... but to the world. If you allow her to present you to My Father, He will give you back to the world. The world needs you, (whispering) the world needs you! I love you!
Notes & Reflections:

JANUARY 5, 1989
MESSAGE FROM OUR LADY

My dear children, my Jesus carried His cross for you. I am now asking you to help Him by carrying your cross for Him. It shall be your joy and your strength. Trust emphatically in Jesus. Trust Him, as He trusts you.

Rejoice in His goodness, and pray in thanksgiving for His mercy. Pray, my dear ones, pray! Thank you for responding to my call.
Notes & Reflections:

JANUARY 5, 1989
MESSAGE FROM OUR LADY

My dear children, thank you for coming. So many of you are responding to my call. You truly are my children, and I thank you for your prayers. I speak to you tonight of trust. Trust Jesus with all of your heart. Some of you are not yet trusting enough. Trust Him with everything. I did, and I am the most blessed of all humanity. My Jesus trusted His Father right up to the time He was poured out, and Jesus became our Saviour.

My dear children, I know it is difficult for you, but you have nothing to fear in trusting Jesus. He will not hurt you. He has sent me to you to be your model of trust. Let this be your goal for this year... trust Jesus with everything. You will not be disappointed. My Son is never outdone in His love. Pour out your hurts to Him. Allow Him to bless you; you who have responded and are part of my prayer group. My dear ones, I, who trust you with my heart, ask you to trust me so that together we will continue to trust Jesus.
Notes & Reflections:

JANUARY 12, 1989
MESSAGE FROM OUR LADY

My dear, dear children, when you allow Jesus to soften your hearts, His heart radiates with such beauty in you! When you open your hearts, Jesus unites His heart with yours. It is so beautiful, and my heart overflows with joyful tears. Thank you for inviting Jesus to soften your hearts. He wishes for you to be the jewels of His crown. Thank you, my dear ones.

Notes & Reflections:

JANUARY 12, 1989
MESSAGE FROM OUR LORD

You are hearing My voice, and I ask you not to harden your hearts. You heard these words from scripture. The people harden their hearts against My Father and they harden their hearts against Me. I am now coming again to you to plead with you; harden not your hearts! You pray that you would hear the word from God, the message from God. Now that you are hearing it, you still do not believe! Harden not your hearts... let them be open to Me, and I will give you what you ask... but you ask with unbelieving hearts. You test Me. I plead with you, My children, do not test Me any longer. The time of doubt is gone! The time of wondering is ceased! Now is the time to listen... open your hearts. If you do not, they will remain hardened, and then even I, your Lord, cannot do anything for you.

This, My dear children, is the power you hold over your Lord and God. Do not hold it over Me any longer for I want to love you and heal you and strengthen you. Listen to My words. Listen to the words of My mother, whom I send you. Now is the time, dear ones. Please allow Me and My mother to soften your hearts. You ask and ask... and do not give! Give Me yourself and then ask what you will of Me, and I can do nothing but give it to you.

I want so much to love you. Please allow Me to love you. It breaks My heart to see hardened hearts. (whisper... weeping audible) I died for those hearts. Give them back to Me.

Notes & Reflections:

JANUARY 19, 1989
MESSAGE FROM OUR LADY

My dear ones, the Lord is with me and, as He is with me, I bring Him to you. I give you my Jesus to love you, and to bless you, and to give you His grace. You are accepting Him; you allow Him to accomplish within you what He wishes.

I am full of grace because of the Lord's will. I offer that grace, my dear ones, to you this night. Thank you for accepting this grace; thank you for accepting His love. Because you love Him so, my love for you grows ever deeper. Thank you for responding to my Jesus. My mission is accomplished... (long pause... then, sadly, slowly, softly) and now my plan (pause again)... can begin.

Notes & Reflections:

JANUARY 20, 1989
MESSAGE FROM OUR LORD

My dear people, it is because of your open hearts I am slow to anger and tender of heart. When you are tender of heart, your love spreads like wild flowers. When you harden your hearts, My flowers turn to weeds.

Every day you have the choice to open your hearts or close them. As you continue to open your heart, I continue to bind special graces from My heart to yours. As soon as you close your hearts and your minds, the transmission is no longer possible. That is why you are advised to pray for the Holy Spirit to sanctify you and to open your hearts. Please, My dear ones, do not despair. Simply center on Me, and remain open-hearted.

Notes & Reflections:

JANUARY 25, 1989
MESSAGE FROM OUR LADY

My dear children, I, your blessed mother, tell you that you are my blessed children! Live in my Son. You, His holy people, can live one with Him in His peace. Do not see me, your mother, as more blessed than you. All, who live in my Jesus are blessed as I. It is possible, through the consecration of my Son's Heart to yours. To live one with my Son in His Kingdom, you can only be blessed, because my Son is blessed.

I, your mother, am blessed, because I live one with Him in His Kingdom. I am purified from sin, because He lives in me. If you will allow Jesus to live in you, you can be purified of sin. He, through His love for you, is inviting you to be His blessed people, living in His peace by loving one another, and centering on Him. My Jesus is tangible, as I am tangible, and We are here for you to grasp on to Us and live in Our hearts.

Notes & Reflections:

FEBRUARY 9, 1989
MESSAGE FROM OUR LORD

My dear people, this is the time of My Divine mercy... accept it graciously. Accept it humbly. What is Divine mercy? It is the power of My Divine love in the Oneness of My Father and Spirit, flowing out from Me on to you... love, which is poured out from My Heart, into your hearts.

I love you, My dear ones. Thank you for your respect and love for My mother. I assure you, it is Me you are loving and respecting, for We are inseparable. We are One, as you and I are one. Thank you, and welcome to the age of My Divine mercy.

Notes & Reflections:

FEBRUARY 16, 1989
MESSAGE FROM OUR LADY

My dear children, I, your mother, ask you to join with me these next forty days in denying yourself for the glory of my Son. Give your love to others. Pass on your love and your mercy. Deny yourself, so that others can have. Join with me. I, your mother, will be denying myself with you for my Son's glory.

Will you please join with me in preparation for the celebration of His resurrection? Have mercy on me by having mercy on my Son, and love His people, my children, your brothers. Thank you for responding to my plea.

Notes & Reflections:

FEBRUARY 23, 1989
MESSAGE FROM OUR LADY

My dear children, tonight I ask you, once again, for total consecration to my Immaculate Heart. I wish to lead you on to the path of holiness. It is the holiness that shines with light, and with infinite mercy. Consecrate yourself daily, so that your abandonment to my Son's will may be made complete. Thank you my dear ones. My blessings and the blessings of my Son, Jesus, pour upon you this night and always.

Notes & Reflections:

FEBRUARY 23, 1989
MESSAGE FROM OUR LORD

Children, I have risen from the dead. The gospel has been fulfilled, and yet, there are so many who do not believe.

It is true... even when My Father raised Me to life, people did not believe, and they still do not. My dear ones, you do believe. I invite you, I beg you, to show your belief in your actions.

Be grateful and hope-filled, so that the ones who are lost will come back. Show My resurrection in your very selves, My dear ones. I love you, and I thank you for living My resurrection. Maybe they will listen to you, and be saved!

Notes & Reflections:

MARCH 2, 1989
MESSAGE FROM OUR LORD

My dear ones, you give Me so much comfort through My passion. Your hearts are so soft, now, that I can mold them into loving hearts. Oh, My people, the joy that you give Me this night is deep, and will last.

The only sign that you ask is to find a new life, which I constantly give you. Thank you for your comfort. Thank you for growing in your realization of how I love you. Truly, it is for you that I died. And with your love, and by your homage, I know that I did not die in vain.

When all children will be as you are, humble, as My people, they will pray with Me to My Eternal Father. How I long for all of them. I thank you again for comforting Me. You truly are the joy of My heart, and I love you.

Notes & Reflections:

MARCH 2, 1989
MESSAGE FROM OUR LADY

My dear children, oh, how happy I am with your openness! Each one of you here is crucial to my plan. My plan is simple. I am working to bring salvation to my children, by opening their hearts to my Son's merciful love and saving grace.

You, my dear ones, are my instruments on earth through which I shall bring glory and praise to my beloved Son and Saviour. Do not speculate as to the details of my plan. Pray that your hearts may be more open to the special graces I wish to give you, and that my Son has allowed.

Once again, my children, I thank you for responding to my motherly call. You, who have said "yes," are my joy in these days.

Notes & Reflections:

MARCH 9, 1989
MESSAGE FROM OUR LADY

My dear ones, tonight I must remind each of you to remain focused on my dear Son. It is true, I am here in a special way, and it is in joy that I thank my Son for allowing it. But children, I am here to announce Jesus, and to call my children back to Him. This is what I ask of you: "Live for my Son, pray to my Son, love my Son and spread His good news." In doing this, my dear ones, you give me great joy. Thank you for responding to my call.

Notes & Reflections:

MARCH 9, 1989
MESSAGE FROM OUR LORD

My dear ones, Moses, who was the servant of My Eternal Father, begged for mercy for his people, and My Father listened. How much more does My Eternal Father listen to Me and to My most beloved mother, when we beg for mercy upon you.

You have My Word in your heart. You have My mother's word, who is with you during these last days of Lent. Devote yourselves, My dear ones, to pleading for mercy, and I, your

Saviour, Who loves you beyond words, will take your cry for mercy to the throne of My Father, and He will listen to Me, just as I listen to My mother.

My dear ones, you must continue to listen to her. She speaks for Me most tenderly. Know that We are with you. You have nothing to fear. My heart glows with love for you. I have poured out mercy upon each of you this night.
Notes & Reflections:

MARCH 16, 1989
MESSAGE FROM OUR LORD

My dear children, I am giving you My mother. I know that you will cherish her, as I. I know that you will love her with all of your heart, as I. I know that you have given her your heart, as I have given her Mine. She and I are of one heart. When you go to her, you come to Me, and so I say, again, come to Me through her. When you are weary, come to Me through her. When you need healing, she will be and already is, My presence to you. Ask for the love that I wish to give to you, and I will give it through her. She is so dear to Me. She constantly says to you about Me... "Listen to Him; do whatever He tells you." Now I, your Lord and Master, tell you, "Do whatever she tells you." She, again, one more time, is speaking for Me.

She, My dear ones, is My prophet to you in these days, in these last days. She speaks for Me. Listen with your heart. There is nothing to fear now. Put your hand in hers, and she will lead you to Me. Be at peace, be at peace, be at peace.
Notes & Reflections:

MARCH 29, 1989
MESSAGE FROM OUR LADY

My dear children, with the resurrection of my Son your purity is restored. It is this day that I dedicate His goodness to you in His purity. It is today that I dedicate myself to you. It is today I celebrate with you in preparation of His feast, the feast of my Son's Divine mercy.

It is because of His goodness and His purity that we are made pure and are invited to be His guests at His feast. Pray in thanksgiving for His goodness, His Divinity, which He wishes to share with you! Thank you, my dear ones, for responding to His call.
Notes & Reflections:

MARCH 30, 1989
MESSAGE FROM OUR LORD

My dear children, from this night on, I give you My mother in the form of this statue. Dedicate yourselves to her. It is a beautiful work, done by My son, Carlos, who is dear to My heart. She cherishes you, My dear ones, as I cherish you. Know of My mercy flowing through her.

This is the time of My mercy. These years will be years of mercy and grace from Me through her. I give you truth, hope, joy, charity, strength, faith, love, and compassion. Treat them with your love. Support them with your strength. My dear ones, I will be sending to you people who will be in need of these virtues, and who will be in need of your mercy. Give them your mercy freely.

My mother loves you. This is her place of grace. She and I are One. When you cherish her, you cherish Me. Know that as she is with you, I am with you, too. Do not fear any longer. The new day has dawned, and with My resurrection, each of you whom I have called here this night, is reborn. Welcome, My newborn babes!

Come to your mother, represented in this statue. When you are weak, come here and she will strengthen you. When you are fearful, come here and take her hand. When you are doubtful, come here and she will lead you to Me. She is the way to My heart. I love her, and I love you and I give her to you. Cherish her as I cherish her.

Notes & Reflections:

APRIL 5, 1989
MESSAGE FROM OUR LADY

My dear children, it pleases me so to be able to speak my messages to you. Know, my dear ones, that all that is happening is true! It is not your imagination! My Son wishes to save His people and you are called to be the instruments of His masterpiece. It is like an orchestra. What beautiful music is created when all the instruments are tuned and played with precision. For all are necessary in the masterpiece of art.

You are my Son's instruments and have been preparing for the grand gala! How wonderful you are and so dear to my heart. Thank you for your obedience and constant devotion to Our divine preparation.

Notes & Reflections:

APRIL 6, 1989
MESSAGE FROM OUR LORD

My dear ones, My beloved children! I beg you, I your Lord, not to ration the Spirit that My Father gives you. Please do not hesitate in your journey. Obey God... whatever the cost! I want so very much to be at the heart of your life. I thank you for your attempt.

Please, My dear ones, do not grow tired in putting Me at the center of your lives. Be bold as you live out the command that I give you, and I will be bold for you with My Father. Use the gifts that My Father's Spirit has given you, and bring My people back to Me. Please do not waste any more time. You live as if you have not said yes! Say "yes" again this night. Please, believe when I say to you, your "yes" is crucial to My plan, which is My mother's plan.

I love you, and I am with you. There is nothing... nothing you need to fear now. Live in My peace, and bring My people home by the example of your obedience and abandonment to

Me. I give you My mother. Know that she pleads for you constantly, and We listen to her prayers.
Notes & Reflections:

APRIL 13, 1989
MESSAGE FROM OUR LORD

My dear ones, I am drawing you nearer to My Father. I ask that you continue to allow Me to draw you to Him. It is a joy for Me, your Lord, to present you to My Father. Continue, dear ones, to respond. Devote yourself to following My mother's call to you to pray. Pray with your heart!

As I present you to My Father, I invite you to give Him everything. Dear ones, please, keep nothing back. If you give Him everything, He will give you life forever. Thank you for your goodness and for your generous hearts. Continue on the path. Resist the temptation to wander from the path. Take My mother's hand. She will never lead you away from the path to My Father, but will be your guide. I love you, thank you.
Notes & Reflections:

APRIL 17, 1989
MESSAGE FROM OUR LADY

My dear children, it is such a blessing for my Jesus to be allowed by His Father to teach you as He taught in His age. It is truly a blessing. He has lessons for you to help you realize the truth, His truth, and the way of guaranteed eternal life with Him. Soon you will be able to read His words to you.

Please do not take lightly my Son's lessons. He wishes for you to be happy and at peace, resting in His Spirit. Know how blessed you are that He speaks to you and is allowed to teach you through the grace of His Father. Rejoice, my dear ones, and begin to practice His ways. Thank you for responding to my call.
Notes & Reflections:

APRIL 20, 1989
MESSAGE FROM OUR LORD

My dear ones, you have accepted Me. You do accept Me, and I thank you for that. My Eternal Father allows Me to speak to you words of hope and challenge.

It is time now to put the words I speak, and have spoken to you, into practice in your daily lives. I am choosing you as My new people. As you say yes, there will be more and more that you will understand, and that will become clearer to you. I want to say to you this night: "My way is simple!" My dear ones, you cause yourselves much pain when you complicate My way. Again I invite you to offer all things to Me, and I will offer them to My Father. Again I remind you, I have sent you My mother. Please allow her to do what she wants with

you, and that is to lead you to Me, so that I can present you to My Father. Live in My Peace. My mercy is upon you.
Notes & Reflections:

APRIL 27, 1989
MESSAGE FROM OUR LADY

My dear children, I, your mother, come to you this evening in hope that you will desire to grasp on to my love for my Son, Who wishes only good things for you. Love Him, my dear ones. Love Him with all of your heart. Do not be afraid of Jesus. He is all good and pure and is your security. Love Him as He loves you. Join your hearts with mine and let us praise our everlasting King!

Do not despair; your prayers are heard! Do not panic for We are with you. Let us simply give praise to my Son in thanksgiving for His wondrous works. Join me this day, my dear ones, to thank my Son. Rejoice with me in my Son, Our Lord, for He is your God. He is my Son and I give Him to you!
Notes & Reflections:

APRIL 27, 1989
MESSAGE FROM OUR LORD

My dear ones, I am your Jesus of Mercy! I invite you to come to Me, and I, if you will allow it, will shed My mercy upon you. My gift to you is My love through My mercy. I ask you to open your hearts and to accept this gift.
Notes & Reflections:

MAY 1, 1989
MESSAGE FROM OUR LADY
FOR THE PARISH

My dear children, today I ask you again to consecrate yourselves to Us! I ask you to trust Us with all, and to pray from your heart. My children, do not have any fears for We are with you. You are precious to Us! Do not give up... Pray! Pray! Pray!

My children, cleanse your hearts so that We might dwell in their purity. My dear children, trust in my Jesus. Ask my Jesus to help you, to strengthen you, to lead you to the Father. All of your prayers are heard and all are answered. My dear children, please open your hearts. Pray with all of your strength, your will, your soul and your mind. Allow my Jesus to fill your hearts with His peace. Thank you for responding to His call.
Notes & Reflections:

MAY 3, 1989
MESSAGE FROM OUR LADY

My dear children, I love you so dearly and wish only to share my Son's purity and glory with you. He loves you, as I, and We give you Our hearts united with Our Father. My Jesus was exalted high, and He wishes you also to rise to eternal glory. Rejoice, my children, for where He is, so you shall be with Him!

Thank God for my Jesus. Thank you God. For my Son is One with Him, and He is your living God for eternity.
Notes & Reflections:

MAY 4, 1989
MESSAGE FROM OUR LORD

My dear children, this is the seedbed where you will be nurtured and strengthened and trained. Then, when you are ready, I will send you out.

Please, children, My special ones, do not doubt Me. You are so like My apostles. On My ascension day, they still doubted and were afraid. I, on this Ascension Day, remind you again, you need not fear! Please do not doubt. Your doubt hurts Me.

I do know, My dear children, what I do to glorify My Eternal Father. Please use this time to be strengthened and nurtured and taught. I will send you out from here. My mother loves you, and is with you each step of your way.
Notes & Reflections:

MAY 11, 1989
MESSAGE FROM OUR LADY

My dear children, I, your mother, wish to thank you for trying so hard to serve my Jesus. Continue to open your hearts daily and allow His divine presence to dwell in your so tender hearts. Pray, pray, my children, for His Spirit to guide you. Center on my Jesus and you will find His truth and His peace.
Notes & Reflections:

MAY 17, 1989
MESSAGE FROM OUR LADY

My dear children, pray to my Jesus, and He shall give to you and comfort you! Accept Him totally as your Lord, God. Know that He can bring you happiness and peace. Trust in my Son! Trust in Him! Be one with Him by giving Him glory and trusting in Him. Pray for peace, my children. Pray! Trust and pray for His peace. Thank you for responding to my call.
Notes & Reflections:

MAY 25, 1989
MESSAGE FROM OUR LADY

My dear children, it pleases me so when you come with open hearts to give glory to my Son. It is in this action of prayer I am able to sing joyfully for you to my Son. How happy I am this day to sing your praises to Him, Who so much desires your love. Do not despair! Have hope, for it is in hope and trust that all goodness shall be delivered to you.

Thank you, my children. Please continue in your journey with me by remaining open hearted, patient and ever so loving. Trust in my Son and you shall be delivered into His Divine hands! Bless you and be at peace.

Notes & Reflections:

JUNE 1, 1989
MESSAGE FROM OUR LADY

My dear children, I ask of you today not to allow yourself to drift during prayer. Pray ever so hard! Please... Pray! Pray! Pray! Focus on my Son. See His face in your heart. My children, you do not realize the glory to be given through my Son. Please center on Him. HE IS HERE FOR YOU... EACH ONE OF YOU. Thank you for responding to my call.

Notes & Reflections:

JUNE 1, 1989
MESSAGE FROM OUR LORD

My dear ones, tonight I am with you to ask each of you: "What do you want Me to do for you?" My dear ones, why are you still afraid of Me? I will never hurt you. I want only your true happiness. Do not be afraid of Me. Please come to Me.

What do you want Me to do for you? Tell Me this night with all of your heart, and I will give you your heart's desire! I invite you again to become closer to My mother so that I can be closer to you. If you are still afraid of Me, don't be afraid of her! Come to her, and she will ease your fear and bring you to Me. I do not want to be distant from you any longer.

Please allow Me, your Lord, this grace. Open your hearts to Me. I want so much to be with you and in you. That is the desire of My heart. That is what you can do for Me. I will always love you.

Notes & Reflections:

JUNE 8, 1989
MESSAGE FROM OUR LORD

My dear ones, you are living now in the reign of My Father. It is here with you now, if you look within and begin living the love that He has offered to you through Me. My blest ones of you, who are living the sacramental life of marriage, live it, My children, with all of your heart. It is the blessed gift of My Father and a sign of His continuing love for you. Cherish one another. Live in My love. Rededicate yourselves to the selflessness of My love in this sacrament.

I bless you, My dear ones, who have been called to the sacrament of marriage. As you live that love, you will be a sign to this world that has forgotten the meaning of self-sacrificing love. If you, My dear ones, love My Father above all else, you will love one another because in one another you will find Him and Myself and Our Holy Spirit! I give you My blessing this night to grow and to prosper, not for yourselves alone, but for this world. Thank you for saying yes to this sacrament.

Notes & Reflections:

JUNE 15, 1989
MESSAGE FROM OUR LADY

My dear children, when you pray with all your heart to my Jesus, focusing on Him, you receive His glory because you are glorifying Him. When you do not drift in prayer, my Jesus is able to dwell in you and your deepest desires and needs can be answered. I know it is not easy for you, my dear ones, but know everything is possible through my Son. Concentrate and practice my Son's goodness and you will grow in His holiness. You will obtain His peace, which He wishes you to have. Thank you, my dear ones, for responding to my call.

Notes & Reflections:

JUNE 15, 1989
MESSAGE FROM OUR LADY

My children, I am here. Thank you for inviting me. My dear ones, I wish for you to continue to remain open hearted. I have spoken of this often because it is so important. Remember you have the choice every day to open your hearts. Please do so daily. Do not come with open hearts on Thursdays only! Remain open hearted when you leave for your homes and make the commitment daily to be open-hearted to my Son. He will fill you with His love.

My married ones, do not argue with your spouse, especially over your beliefs. Love, do not argue. It is your love and your actions which shall draw my dear ones to my Son... not your words! Love, pray, and please, I urge you, remain open hearted so that you will be prepared! Thank you for your response to my call.

Notes & Reflections:

JUNE 22, 1989
MESSAGE FROM OUR LADY

My dear children, once again I am here with you. Whenever you open your hearts to my Son, you can be sure that I am in your presence, because you allow me.

This week, my children, I ask of you to begin fasting for my Jesus. There are many ways to fast. Go slowly and do not attempt to fast on bread and water if you have not fasted before! You are to be happy when you fast, not gloomy and do not let your peers know you are fasting! Simply do so joyfully. If you begin to fast and pray, I shall help you so your fasting becomes natural. Do not fast more than two times a week! If you cannot fast on bread and water, then delete something of your pleasure and offer it to my Son.

Bless you, my children, and do not fear! Offer everything up to my Son tonight, and He shall purify and comfort you. Thank you once again, for your response to my call.
Notes & Reflections:

JUNE 22, 1989
MESSAGE FROM OUR LORD

My dear ones, I again, tonight, give you My mother as the new Eve as I, your Lord, am the new Adam.

You are Our children through My love and through the water which came from My side. You have been adopted at a great price. The sign that you are Our children is forgiveness.

My Father wants to forgive you. I plead for you. My mother pleads for you. My children, please begin to forgive. That will open your heart! In your generosity of love, go deep within your heart to ask forgiveness, and the grace to forgive.

I and My Father give Mary to you again tonight. Do not ignore her or her invitation to you. Take her hand again this night, and journey in forgiveness to Me, so that I can take you to Our Father.

If, My dear ones, you need a reminder of forgiveness, look upon Myself nailed to the cross. I loved you then and I still love you! Allow Me to love you more, as you forgive more. My peace is with you now.
Notes & Reflections:

JUNE 24, 1989
MESSAGE FROM OUR LADY
TO PEACE CENTER DAY OF RECOLLECTION

My dear children, my heart overflows with joy! I am with you again this day! Pray that you will be able to remain open to my Jesus... to all of the graces He wishes to bestow upon you!

My dear children, pray with your whole heart... pray constantly. Never cease in your prayers! Your prayers are heard and ALL are answered! Thank you for responding to my call.
Notes & Reflections:

JUNE 24, 1989
MESSAGE FROM OUR LORD
TO PEACE CENTER DAY OF RECOLLECTION

My dear people, eight years ago My mother asked permission in a last effort to make known to My people, how much they are loved, and to ask for your hearts. It has been eight years that I have allowed her to convert you, My people.

It is because of your prayers and love that I remain tender-hearted as she brings you to Me. I now have allowed My mother to continue and to be here with you. We both, together, are here in the Americas, to gather Our people in love.

Be prepared, My dear ones, for the many to come here! Be open-hearted and ready to accommodate. I am here to save and to destroy evil, so all may live in My goodness and dwell in My Kingdom. It is My Divinity I wish to share with you, My jewels of My crown. There is nothing I shall keep from you.

You are My people and many more shall come to this, My center of Mercy! My mother has chosen her children, and I have chosen My one of love and mercy! They are symbols for this world to live by. They are symbols of truth, faith, hope, joy, strength, compassion, charity, humility, courage and My one of love and mercy. See these, my children, as examples for which you are to live.

As you celebrate the anniversary of My mother's 8th year, celebrate your first year anniversary! There shall be many more to come. It is not the end, My people, but the beginning!

Prepare! Go in My peace and know We are with you.

Notes & Reflections:

JUNE 29, 1989
MESSAGE FROM OUR LORD

I have had so much hope for you, My dear ones, and now I come to you and I, your Lord, plead with you... embrace your cross.

Do you think it was easy for Me to bear the cross for you? I gladly did it for love of you and in obedience to My Father. I beg you... embrace your cross in reparation for your sins.

You have no idea how your sins continue to grieve Me! I love you! Please love Me! I want you with Me. You need to make reparation for your sins.

My mother grieves for you and pleads for you. The time is truly short. I beg you... listen to Me or listen to My mother... but, LISTEN! My Eternal Father has sent Us to you! I died in love! Please, My dear ones, live for Me in reparation for your sins and in love. I promise to be with you always.

Notes & Reflections:

JULY 6, 1989
MESSAGE FROM OUR LADY

My dear children, I, your mother, tell you there is no time to waste in your conversion. Please, open your hearts to my Son and pray with all your might to Him for the salvation of this world. Do not be fearful. There is no time for fear! Be strong soldiers, faithful ones, and begin living in His purity. I cannot stress enough to you the importance of these words!

Please begin acting as pure soldiers, my angels of love. Put aside your personal desires and seek the desire of my Son. I am here for a purpose. That purpose is to bring you to Him, and to save you... only this! Thank you, my dear ones, for responding to my call. Our peace is with you.

Notes & Reflections:

JULY 6, 1989
MESSAGE FROM OUR LADY

It gives me great joy to be with you this night as you honor my Son under the title of His Mercy. Ask Him and Our Eternal Father to be with you. My Jesus under His title of mercy will also be here! Come to Him, my dear ones. My heart overflows with joy at how much He loves, and how much He loves you, each of you!

Our Eternal Father has allowed both of Us to be with you. This will be a center of my Jesus' mercy for all who come. As they come, my dear ones, whether you understand or not, you are prepared to receive all of these ones. Have mercy on them, and my Jesus will have mercy on you. He is shedding His mercy upon you now. As you come to Him, do not fear to hope, for He has great hope for you!

I take you, my dear ones, into my heart this night and present you to my Jesus of Mercy with His heart overflowing with love and forgiveness for those who ask! We will always be with you until the time when We come to take you home! Until that time, know that this is your home, because this is where His mercy and my peace dwell for you. Thank you for honoring my Son. Thank you, my dear ones. Peace! Peace!

Notes & Reflections:

JULY 13, 1989
MESSAGE FROM OUR LADY

My dear children, one year ago I asked several children if they would deny themselves for my Son's glory and suffer much ridicule. They responded joyfully to His service. For one year now I have been preparing them and molding them to be the leaders of my army of which you are all a part.

You must know that these children are not more special than you, but that I and my Son selected them to carry out Our commands because of their youth, strength and energy! Know you are all chosen and are my children, my Son's people. These children have been given symbols which you are to live by and have been given many special graces of discernment, spiritual healings, emotional healings and physical healings. In addition, one of these children has been selected by my Son as a source through which His Divine radiance and mercy shall flow out onto many. These children shall soon be made known to you for they are at the end of their preparation.

My dear children, know We are not asking you to change your way of life, but to change your heart so that your lives can be lived in happiness. My Jesus wishes for you to be His chosen ones. All who desire Him are chosen! Thank you, my dear ones, and please, support my children with your love! I tell you they are working on your behalf for your salvation! My peace be with you.

Notes & Reflections:

JULY 20, 1989
MESSAGE FROM OUR LADY

My dear children, first always seek the Kingdom of God. Live your lives in the holiness of my Son and seek His Kingdom. I tell you, if you do not seek the Kingdom of God, your prayers are in vain! He is the truth and all your works should be done to His pleasure. Seek the Kingdom of God first, above all. Thank you, my dear ones, for responding to my call.

Notes & Reflections:

JULY 20, 1989
MESSAGE FROM OUR LORD

My dear ones, I, your Lord, do offer you this night My comfort and My peace. The words of My gospel message are true. My yoke is easy and My burden light, because I never give you a task, a cross, or a burden, without also being there with you every step of your way!

My dear ones, **I AM YOUR WAY!** Allow Me to journey with you, and you will be free and peace-filled. I offer you life... My life! I invite you to accept that gift. Come to Me as you are weary, and I truly will give you refreshment. Come to Me when you feel lonely, and I will be with you.

You give Me so much joy! You are responding. Continue to respond in love, no matter how difficult the road. I am with you, and I give you My mother, also. Take Our hand, and We will lead you to the Kingdom of My Father!

Notes & Reflections:

JULY 27, 1989
MESSAGE FROM OUR LORD

My dear children, today I again, give you My mother. She is My love and My breath! I give you her because you are her loved ones, and her breath of desire. Allow her to be your love and your breath!

She is so beautiful, and is all that I am! Give her honor. When you give her honor, you are giving Me and My Father honor. Our honor will result in your glory! Thank you for your faith in Our truth. Peace, and My blessings to you.

Notes & Reflections:

AUGUST 3, 1989
MESSAGE FROM OUR LADY

My dear children, receive my Son through His Eucharist. Receive Him and invite Him to purify, dwell and rest in you.

My children, you do not realize the power of my Jesus in His Eucharist. It is He... in physical form, My Son, your Jesus, the manna of life! Please, receive Him and allow Him to make you holy! Thank you, my children, for responding to my call.

Notes & Reflections:

AUGUST 10, 1989
MESSAGE FROM OUR LADY

My dear children, this week I invite you to ask my Spouse, the Holy Spirit, to dwell in you and guide you. All you need to do is ask Him to dwell in you at the beginning of each morning. He shall watch over you, and you shall see His wondrous works as He guides you this week in your daily lives. There is something for all of you!

PLEASE, do not forget to invite Him daily! PLEASE, invite the Holy Spirit to dwell in you.

Thank you, my dear ones, for your response to my call.

Notes & Reflections:

AUGUST 10, 1989
MESSAGE FROM OUR LORD

My dear ones, My dear mother is honored by Myself and by My Father, because of her obedience. This obedience did not come from her human understanding, but from her Spouse, Our Holy Spirit.

I give her to you this night as an example of the kind of obedience I invite you to give to Me, and to her, and to Our heavenly Father. Because of her obedience, she was able to pray: "My soul magnifies the Lord, and my spirit rejoices in God, my Saviour."

My dear ones, the gift of your obedience is the gift of your heart to Me. When you obey Me, I take that gift and present it to My Father. It is because of your obedience that many, many graces are being shed upon you at this place at this time. And because of your obedience, you are causing that grace to overflow onto all those who come to you!

My Father allows Me to come to thank you for your obedience. I take you into My heart again, this night, in gratitude for that gift; and I leave My mother with you as My physical sign and example to you of the obedience that is most pleasing to My Father. Continue, My dear ones, to cherish her as she so cherishes you! You are allowing her, because of your obedience, to lead you to Me. I give you My mercy and My love. Live on in My peace.

Notes & Reflections:

AUGUST 15, 1989
MESSAGE FROM OUR LORD
FEAST OF THE ASSUMPTION

My dear people, on this, My mother's feast, I wish to share with you My joy, as I celebrate in her goodness, as the mother of humankind. Lift your voices and give praise and honor to My mother, for she is your mother, as I have given her to you. My people, celebrate and open your hearts to her love. Her love grants you your salvation!

Be at peace, and know I have gathered your prayers to My most compassionate heart, and shall answer them according to your intimate happiness. Bless you, My people, My peace I give you.

Notes & Reflections:

AUGUST 17, 1989
MESSAGE FROM OUR LORD

My dear ones, Our Holy Spirit has been always with you from the very beginning of your time here on earth, prompting you, guiding you, protecting you and sanctifying you. Our Spirit was the gift We gave you, and it is the gift that I give you again this night!

Receive again, Our Holy Spirit. **Through that Spirit, I your Lord, touch your heart this night.** Allow Me to melt your heart if it is closed and cold. Allow Me to open it, and to pour My mercy this night upon you. Give Me your heart, and I will take it and put it in My heart, and there Our Father will see you in Me. My dear ones, allow this blessing to happen! Give Me that gift, so that My mercy and the gift of Our Holy Spirit may flow to you, healing, forgiving and sanctifying.

I love you. I will always love you! I, your Lord, will never give up on you... NEVER, NEVER, NEVER!

Notes & Reflections:

AUGUST 31, 1989
MESSAGE FROM OUR LADY

My dear little children, you are my holy ones! I thank you for your prayers, and I invite you this night to more prayer. Honor my Son with your prayer. Pray for peace, please. Pray that your heart may continue to be converted.

I see your weariness, little ones. Please, I invite you not to give up, but to continue in your prayer. Your prayer is so vital to me and for your world. DON'T GIVE UP. CONTINUE! Believe me when I say it is because of your prayer that I, your mother, am allowed to be with you in so many ways for so long a time. This, truly, is the time of my Son's grace. Never stop allowing Him to work through you. I promise, little ones, to come whenever you invite me! It is the joy of my heart when you invite me, your mother, to pray with you to my Son and our Saviour, Jesus. Thank you for your prayers and for trying so hard to love! Your attempts do not go unnoticed. Thank you, my little ones, my little holy ones. I love you!

Notes & Reflections:

AUGUST 31, 1989
MESSAGE FROM OUR LADY

My dear children, once again I ask you to take prayer seriously. In these days Satan is trying to cause much harm and disrupt your peace. Please pray with all your heart and take prayer seriously. Do not speak of my messages only. Please, begin to absorb them and live them! Remember, it is not what you say but what you do! Prayer will bring you to my Jesus and is your protection from Satan. Please pray continuously and know I cannot give you any new messages until you begin to live the current ones! I love you, my dear ones, and I am praying for you. Thank you for your response to my call.

Notes & Reflections:

SEPTEMBER 7, 1989
MESSAGE FROM OUR LADY

My dear children, today is the day on which I ask you to fight Satan by loving and accepting one another. Satan cannot and will not win! Love slays him.

Be strong and accept one another. Much glory will be given to you who persevere. Please trust in God. Please seek God and put aside your sentiments and emotions. Please do not argue with one another. All are beautiful in God's eyes. Seek His Kingdom and fight Satan through loving and accepting one another! Thank you for your response to my call.

Notes & Reflections:

SEPTEMBER 7, 1989
MESSAGE FROM OUR LORD

My dear ones, why don't you trust in My care for you? I extend always My mercy and love to you. My Father sent Me to you, not to frighten you, but only to love you. Why do you still hesitate to trust? I ask for your obedience. Is it such a difficult request? I long for your heart. Can't you see that when you give Me your heart, I can fill it with My mercy and love? I long to do that!

I ask you, again, listen and obey, and I will be able to present you to My Father, and flood you with My mercy. I love you with all My heart. I beg you, trust Me!
Notes & Reflections:

SEPTEMBER 14, 1989
MESSAGE FROM OUR LADY

My dear children, It is through the blood of my Son that you, His beloved people, have been redeemed. When you *completely* trust in Him, He is able to cure you, heal you and sanctify you in His Spirit.

Please, my dear, dear children, totally trust in my Son. Allow my tears for your sorrow to cleanse you and purify you. I, your Mother of Sorrows, have lived your sorrow, and am here to comfort you. This is my wish for you: Total happiness and peace in my Son! Thank you, my dear ones, for your response to my call of total trust.
Notes & Reflections:

SEPTEMBER 14, 1989
MESSAGE FROM OUR LORD

My dear ones, I ask you, this night, not to run away from the cross. As you look on My cross, remember My obedience to My Father.

Please, My dear ones, I beg you not to be fearful of the cross! It was the instrument that gave you life and that gave Me life! The cross is to be embraced. It is not to be run from. Embrace My cross in your lives, and know that when you do so, you are embracing Me!

The way of acceptance is THROUGH OBEDIENCE. Obedience leads through death to life. Why else would you celebrate the triumph of an instrument of destruction? Because of My obedience to My Father, He turned the instrument of destruction into the way for life eternal with Him.

My dear ones, I offer you, this night, a share of My cross. For each one of you, it will be manifested in a different way. But it is My Cross! I ask you, accept it! Embrace it! For as you accept it and embrace it, you accept Me and embrace Me. I will be with you. I promise to be with you, as you share with Me the cross of redemption and life.

My cross is the sign of My love for you. Embracing My cross will be a sign of your love for Me, and My Father, Who glorified My cross, will also glorify yours! HE LOVES US SO MUCH.
Notes & Reflections:

SEPTEMBER 21, 1989
MESSAGE FROM OUR LORD

My dear people, in this, my "Age of My Divine Mercy", it is your self-centeredness and soul I have mercy on! It is during this time that I give to you My peace for your devotion to My Father.

The lack of love will continue until My people turn to their God with hope and thanksgiving! I wish for all to be filled with My Spirit of goodness, truth, joy, peace and compassion! I wish for all to receive My love and My mercy. Turn away from your self-righteousness and be righteous in Me, your loving God!

AMEN TO THOSE WHO HEAR MY WORDS AND REJOICE FOR THEY SHALL INHERIT THE LAND OF THE LIVING!
Notes & Reflections:

SEPTEMBER 28, 1989
MESSAGE FROM OUR LADY

My dear children, during this age of my Son's Divine Mercy, He sheds upon each of you His holiness and His Divine Spirit. How blessed you are, my children. You are my Son's blessed people. You are His holy ones. That is why I ask you to persevere, have strength and always remain in your faith. These words are encouragement for you because I know the plan my Jesus has for you! He loves you beyond your deepest recognition. He loves you, my dear children, and I, your mother and mistress, adore Him in your name!

PRAISE BE MY JESUS. HE IS YOUR JESUS OF MERCY!
Notes & Reflections:

OCTOBER 5, 1989
MESSAGE FROM OUR LADY

My dear children, I, your mother, am so pleased to see how you are reconciling with your fellow brothers. I am pleased with your openness and loving embraces. Thank you for your effort, my dear ones.

When you are open, you allow my Jesus to convert your hearts to the way He created them! He is by your side, guiding you, especially in your weakest moments of vulnerability! Continue to walk with Us in openness and honesty. All else shall be taken care of for you!

Remember, a healthy soul overcomes all ailments. Thank you for your response to my call.
Notes & Reflections:

OCTOBER 12, 1989
MESSAGE FROM OUR LADY

My dear children, this night I wish for you to focus on my Son. Do not look at yesterday or anticipate tomorrow. Do not speak of the things and events that cause distraction or harm in your conversion! SPEAK OF THE GOOD AND PEACEFUL EVENTS. DO NOT DWELL ON CHASTISEMENT OR THE EVENTS TO COME. DWELL ON PEACE AND PEACE WILL COME!

You are the instruments through which conversion is seeded in my Son's people, my children. I wish my children to come back to my Son through love and peace, not because fear is instilled in them from what may not come. Speak of goodness and be loving always.

Please, hear and listen to my words with obedience. I wish all of you, who have been converted to my Son's tender heart, to convert others through love and speaking of peace and goodness, as you were called. DO NOT BLOCK YOUR CONVERSION BY DWELLING ON THE INCORRECT SUBJECT! PEACE IS THE SUBJECT, AND LOVE AND MERCY, NOT WARS, DISASTERS, OR THE CHASTISEMENT! Thank you, my dear ones, for responding seriously to this call.
Notes & Reflections:

OCTOBER 12, 1989
MESSAGE FROM OUR LORD

My dear ones, I want to thank you for your persistence in prayer. I say again that not one of your prayers goes unheard, or goes undelivered to My heavenly Father.

I, this night, encourage you to continue in your prayer for peace, for conversion, and for My Divine mercy. Those gifts I gladly give to you so that, in turn, you may give them to My little ones who are still so lost. The desire of My heart is to have all of them with Me.

Please, pray for them, gather them for Me. I use you as My hands and My arms and My heart. Embrace them and it will be Me embracing them! I thank you, and I love you, and I give you My Spirit.
Notes & Reflections:

OCTOBER 19, 1989
MESSAGE FROM OUR LADY

My dear children, always thank God for the many blessings of life He has granted you. Continuously give Him praise and thanks. Contemplate His goodness, for Our Father is a gracious and most loving God.

If Jesus gives to you a life of everlasting happiness and peace, think of the goodness and blessedness of Our God, through Whom all goodness and gifts of beauty are created! Thank Him, for He gave to you the key to everlasting life... His Son, your Jesus! Blessed be Jesus and blessed be His children, created by the Eternal One on High, for they are one with Him!
Notes & Reflections:

OCTOBER 19, 1989
MESSAGE FROM OUR LORD

My dear ones, when you pray for My mercy, as you have done so lovingly this night, it melts My heart. I cannot describe the love that I give to you this night, as you pray for My mercy.

I beg you, My dear ones, do not stop praying for My mercy. It is truly My joy to give it to you, and to all those for whom you pray. My joy overflows upon you this night. The tenderness with which I gather you in My arms is so much like the tenderness that My mother constantly has for you. Your prayers of mercy are answered. You have captured My heart! I love you so.

I ask you now, you who have My mercy, be merciful to all of them whom I send you each day. As they experience My mercy through you, their hearts will likewise be melted and they will no longer be afraid to come to Me themselves. Look at what you have done for Me, your Lord! I thank you and I love you and I give you now, My peace. Know, from this moment on, that My peace is with you always.

My mother sends her love to you this night as she continues to pray with you. Oh, My dear ones, how she and I love you! Remember, however, that Our love is simply the reflection of the love that Our Father, My Father, has for each of you, His adopted loved ones!
Notes & Reflections:

OCTOBER 26, 1989
MESSAGE FROM OUR LADY

My dear children, you are the little children of God. Please use your gifts of faith, trust and hope. They are such powerful graces bestowed upon you in the eyes of God. Please have confidence in Him and trust emphatically.

Your faith is your comfort! The more you trust, the more you shall be comforted! God will care for you. He has all this time, and shall not stop providing.

DO NOT ALLOW ANYONE TO DISRUPT YOUR FOCUS AND TRUST FOR MY SON. Walk with Him and trust with all confidence in His divine care. He shall comfort you through the grace of your faith. Thank you, my little children, for your response to my call, a call for peace and happiness!
Notes & Reflections:

OCTOBER 26, 1989
MESSAGE FROM OUR LORD

My dear ones, I come to you this night to tell you what an effect you have had, and still have, on Me, your Lord. When I came to you the first time, I did not intend to bring dissension, and yet, I saw that the more I spoke the truth, the more the people resisted it. I say to you, I do not come this time to bring dissension, but to bring truth and salvation.

Still, My children look upon Me, their Saviour and upon My Father, Who is their God, with hearts that are not open, because you are still judging, even judging yourself in your relationship with Me! I have called you My friends to show you what freedom I give to you and what respect I have for you, each of you.

PLEASE BELIEVE IN THE VALUE OF YOUR LIFE. PLEASE BELIEVE HOW MUCH I LOVE YOU AND WANT YOU T0 FOLLOW ME. I want you to follow as a friend, not as a slave! I beg you, do not be slaves to the evil one, to your pride, to your selfishness!

I give you My strength and My love to overcome the power of the evil one. I ask you, again this night, to use the power of My Spirit within you, so that you may experience the peace and the joy and the love of My own heart! I want so much for each of you to be in My heart!
Notes & Reflections:

NOVEMBER 9, 1989
MESSAGE FROM OUR LORD

My dear people, love the ones you dislike! When they hurt you, pray for them. I will give you My peace and compassion. With My compassion, you will be able to forgive them and you will have My mercy for them. You will love them with My love, a love which embraces the soul.

I loved My enemies and I still love the ones who do not wish to know Me. It is My compassion that saves them. It is your compassion that will also save your enemies in My name and in My love.

I tell you, the day will come for you, who follow Me, when you will love your enemies with a love you never knew existed! You will love them greater than a dearest friend because it will be My love! Pray for the ones who befriend you. My glory, happiness and peace shall rest with you. Thank you, My beloved ones, and My peace be with you!
Notes & Reflections:

NOVEMBER 23, 1989
MESSAGE FROM OUR LORD

My dear people, know the time of My saving grace is at hand!

My lessons, once available to the world, shall commence My grace period, allowed by My Father to gather My good! The good shall be weeded from the bad for no man gathers fruitless crops from His harvest!

TAKE HEED, MY PEOPLE, AND KNOW OF MY GREAT LOVE FOR YOU. TRUST IN ME!

Trusting in Me is living in Me as one Spirit. Trust in yourselves by trusting in Me as I trust in you! There are many blessings I wish to give to you, many endless gifts which await you, graces of life! Say, "yes" to your Jesus and say, "yes" to eternal life!
Notes & Reflections:

NOVEMBER 30, 1989
MESSAGE FROM OUR LADY

My dear children, I, your mother, invite you again this night, to follow my Son. I encourage you to continue to pray with your hearts. You are seeing in your world the power of prayer! DO NOT GIVE UP! Your prayer, united to mine, is more powerful than Satan!

My dear ones, rededicate yourself, this night, to prayer. My heart is so full of gratitude. I thank you. I love you. I am with you, thanks to the love my Son has for each of you. Be at peace. Receive the grace of my Son.

Notes & Reflections:

NOVEMBER 30, 1989
MESSAGE FROM OUR LADY

My dear children, do not be discouraged. My Jesus is here for you! It is difficult to convince people to accept and trust in my Son's truth, because there are so few who love Him. But do not be discouraged. Your love and actions will set the precedence for their conversion. Simply pray for all and you will be saved! I cannot stress enough to you the seriousness of your prayers.

THE ANTICHRIST IS ALIVE AND WISHES T0 DECEIVE YOU! Pray to my Jesus. He loves you and will protect you. The antichrist is weak and he wishes for you to think that you are weak! Know that all who follow and walk with my Son are powerful because they receive the Father's zeal of power and strength.

Remember, those who walk with my Jesus are not weak. It is the demons who are weak. NEVER, NEVER FORGET WHAT I HAVE TOLD YOU! Peace, my loved ones, and thank you for responding to my call!

Notes & Reflections:

DECEMBER 2, 1989
MESSAGE FROM OUR LORD

I give you My holy mother, My dear ones; this now is her season. I give her to you as the sample of how I invite you to respond to My call.

My dear ones, never think that honoring My mother brings dishonor to Me! WHEN YOU SEE MY MOTHER, YOU SEE ME! How it saddens My heart that so many of My children reject My mother. Don't they know that when they reject her, they are rejecting My heart. I LOVE HER SO!

I invite you to love her, for she loves you with her Immaculate Heart. I rejoice this night because of her, and if I, your Lord, honor her, why do My children not follow My example? Take her hand, honor her, love her, and she will lead you to Me.

I give you My peace. I give you My heart. Cherish these gifts until I return to you.
Notes & Reflections:

DECEMBER 14, 1989
MESSAGE FROM OUR LADY

My dear children, this day my Son has gathered into His most tender heart all of those you have prayed for in love! Prayer is the key to all success. The success of my plan relies on your prayer and devotion to my Son! Please, continue to pray and live in His faith. It will successfully end in your salvation. YOU GAIN HIS POWER THROUGH PRAYER! Thank you, my dear ones, and know I continually pray for you!
Notes & Reflections:

DECEMBER 21, 1989
MESSAGE FROM OUR LADY

My dear children, love your Jesus with all of your heart as He loves you! Take pride in loving His loved ones, for all belong to Him. Love and sincerity are the key to eternal glory. You have the gift of love because you have my Son! Please, use this gift, especially now, during this celebration of His birth. I promise you, your soul will rejoice!

Celebrate with me, for our Saviour is here and He is yours. Rejoice and be glad. Know Him, my dear ones. Know Him intimately, for He is here for each one of you. Peace, my dear ones. Peace for all eternity for you, my children of the Americas!
Notes & Reflections:

DECEMBER 25, 1989
MESSAGE FROM OUR LADY

My dear children, the kings came from afar to pay homage to our King, and today He, your King, comes to bring you hope and happiness. He is your sweet Jesus!

Please, my dear ones, know the way of my Son. Practice His ways and unite with Him. He brings you tidings of joy. Pray, pray, pray to your beloved God of Hosts. Pray, and live according to His way. It is so necessary to receive His graces. Begin once again, this day, my dear ones. Commence the new decade with mercy! Thank you for responding to my call.
Notes & Reflections:

DECEMBER 28, 1989
MESSAGE FROM OUR LADY

My dear children, it is glorious that my Son has allowed me to come here. Live your lives for Him, as I. My dear, dear children, I am your Mother of Mercy - I have come here to the Americas to bring my children back to my Son. His mercy is upon you. I wish for all to be glorified in Him. It is all possible through desire and prayer.

Always pray, and the Divine Father shall replenish you with abundant gifts. Love one another always. Love all of different faiths. Never deny anyone your love, for all belong to the Father! Never condemn! Always, always, love. Be patient and peaceful children. Thank you for responding to my call.

Notes & Reflections:

JANUARY 4, 1990
MESSAGE FROM OUR LORD

My dear loved ones, with all My heart, I invite you to come and to see your Lord! I, Who dwell always in the tabernacle, am always present to you in the tabernacle of the altar and in the tabernacle of your heart! It is My wish, the wish of your Lord, that you would begin to appreciate My real presence in both of those tabernacles!

Please believe Me, My dear ones. I am as truly present in the tabernacle of your heart as I am truly present in the tabernacle of this altar! That is how much I love you. I come to dwell within you, and when I come to dwell within you, I bring with Me My most holy Father and Our most holy Spirit. You are the tabernacle of Our Life! I beg you, My dear ones, to hold sacred, as I do, the tabernacle of your heart.

Treasure My presence within you. I AM ALWAYS WITH YOU. There is nothing at all to be afraid of. Be at peace, and know that I, your Lord, love you and consecrate you to My Father.

Notes & Reflections:

JANUARY 11, 1990
MESSAGE FROM OUR LADY

My dear children, it pleases me to see your hearts devoted to my Son. You love Him dearly. It is my wish now for you to allow my Jesus to love you. It is He Who desires to give to you. Always pray and be open to Him.

In these days, it is so necessary to focus intently on prayer and the love my Son has for you. Live in His faith always and never despair. All that He has promised will be fulfilled! Have faith in what He has told you, for it will be done according to the word of His law! Thank you, my dear ones, for your response to my call.

Notes & Reflections:

JANUARY 11, 1990
MESSAGE FROM OUR LORD

My dear ones, I, your Lord, wish to heal you. I, your Lord, wish to make you whole again. Allow Me that freedom in your heart. I want to tell you how you limit My love for you, how you block what I long to do for you.

COME TO ME WITH OPEN HEART, WITH OPEN MIND. PLACE YOURSELF BEFORE ME IN MY SACRAMENT, AND THEN I WILL BE ABLE TO HEAL YOU AS I WISH!

Please believe Me, please trust in Me, that I, your Lord, know how and when and what you most need healing in! It is My mercy and My love that I wish to pour upon you. These are the healing graces that are yours. If you only allow Me to give them to you!

Present to Me this night your heart, and I will embrace it and draw it nearer to Mine; and there you will feel My mercy and My healing and My love. You will be filled with joy, the joy that I wish to give you. Please, My dear ones, believe Me when I say: "I love you with all of My heart."

Notes & Reflections:

JANUARY 18, 1990
MESSAGE FROM OUR LADY

My dear children, pray in thanksgiving to my Son for allowing me to come here! He is your beloved Master and Saviour. He is the only way to true happiness, peace and comfort. Please, trust in Him.

You are still frightened and wish to control. Trust in my Son! Please, practice His ways and cease your arguments! Be open-hearted and loving people. This is truly necessary in order for you to accommodate the many to come here.

IT IS YOUR LOVE THEY NEED, AND YOUR WELCOME, AS I WELCOME AND LOVE ALL WHO COME TO THIS, MY SON'S CENTER OF MERCY! Jesus has blessed you with me so, please, thank Him by showing others love. Thank you for responding to my call.

Notes & Reflections:

JANUARY 18, 1990
MESSAGE FROM OUR LORD

My dear ones, I beg you, this night, to overcome your jealousy. Don't you realize, that when you are jealous of another, you disregard the gift that My Father has given to you? I tell you again, there is no gift greater than another gift. Each gift comes from My Father.

I ask you this night, allow Me, your Saviour and Lord, to heal jealousy in your heart, so that I can give you a new heart. Rejoice in the gift that I give you, My merciful love. Look upon the gifts of your brothers and sisters and be thankful for them, thankful to the Spirit, thankful to My Father.

I beg you to resign your jealousy, and use the gifts that you have to touch those whom I will send you, if you allow Me. I will give you My mercy for them. It will be My mercy, through you, if you only allow it! Know that I love you and that I want for you joy.
Notes & Reflections:

JANUARY 25, 1990
MESSAGE FROM OUR LADY

My dear children, always be loving, open and honest. This is so necessary in order for you to relay my messages to those who come here, exactly as they are, without adding or subtracting from them. Always be loving, and you shall receive the joy you bring my Son. This joy is endless and brings glory. Thank you, my dear ones, for your response to my call.
Notes & Reflections:

JANUARY 25, 1990
MESSAGE FROM OUR LORD

My dear ones, what I say to you this night, I ask you to listen to carefully. Because you are My disciples, YOU will suffer. Because you are saying, "yes," and allowing My Father and Myself and Our Spirit to convert you, you will suffer.

As you spread our good news of joy, peace and hope to the world, you will be ridiculed. You will be laughed at and you will suffer. I tell you this night, My dear ones, that through all of that suffering, I AM WITH YOU. I SEND MY MOTHER TO BE WITH YOU.

And so I say to you, do not fear suffering because I can take that and redeem many! I thank you for saying, "yes," for taking the risk in believing, in loving, in touching those whom I send to you.

I give you this night a blessing, the sign of My cross on your heart, a sign that contradicted the world. The sign of suffering is turned into eternal joy. This is what I will do with your suffering. I will turn it into joy as you give it to Me. I love you. Bear all!
Notes & Reflections:

FEBRUARY 1, 1990
MESSAGE FROM OUR LADY

My dear children, I invite you to unite in the Oneness of my Son's peace. If you live in my Son's peace, you will accept with obedience all of what I tell you. You will not be resentful or jealous.

I have come for all my children; not a select few. Open your hearts and love all. Unite with my Son and live in His peace. Accept what I tell you with obedience. It is for your divine protection and glory! Thank you, my dear ones, for your response to my call.
Notes & Reflections:

FEBRUARY 1, 1990
MESSAGE FROM OUR LORD

My dear ones, as I sent My disciples long ago, I now send you. I ask you to give, once you have learned here from Me, My mercy, totally, to those around you. I ask you to depend totally upon Me; not upon the gifts I have given you, but upon Me, your Lord, your Jesus of Mercy.

I invite you to come often to Me seeking forgiveness, strength, healing. Come to Me in My Eucharistic presence, and then I will heal you, strengthen you, as you go back to being My disciples of mercy.

This world needs My mercy, and I will give it through you, My dear ones. How you have captured My heart! May you draw closer to My heart this night, and thank you for listening. How happy you make Me when you listen to My words; when I tell you I love you and I am with you as you go to those to whom I send you!
Notes & Reflections:

FEBRUARY 8, 1990
MESSAGE FROM OUR LADY

My dear children, tonight I speak to you, again, of love. Please do not despair. Love all and be at peace with the will of God. Open your hearts daily! **Continually love and accept my Son's peace by accepting His will for you.** Thank you, my dear ones, for your response to my call.
Notes & Reflections:

FEBRUARY 8, 1990
MESSAGE FROM OUR LORD

My dear ones, I come to you tonight to ask you to acknowledge your poverty. I do hear the cry of the poor and I ask you to realize that when you cling on to your own desire, your own will, your own pleasure, you are the poorest of the poor! Because, My dear ones, when you do that, you really reject the gifts that I give you for yourself as your own. Abject poverty of the worst kind is when you do not love yourself. With that kind of poverty always comes judgment and condemnation, not only of others, but of yourself.

I ask you why, in your poverty, you do not acknowledge your poverty? Give that to Me so that I, Who am your Jesus of Mercy, can give you a richer life. I again tonight give you My peace.

I again tell you that I am with you. My hope is that one day you will believe and, as you do, you will be lifted from your poverty. I love you.
Notes & Reflections:

FEBRUARY 15, 1990
MESSAGE FROM OUR LADY

My dear children, tonight I wish to ask you what you are doing for my Son? He gives to you all goodness, and continually gives you gifts. What are you giving Him?

All He asks of you is your heart so that He may fill it with joy. **Please live in obedience and trust in Him.** Give Him the great gift of your heart, and you will be giving Him great honor. It is the greatest gift you could give to yourself, the gift of my Son!

I love you, my dear children, here and throughout the world. Thank you for responding to my call.
Notes & Reflections:

FEBRUARY 22, 1990
MESSAGE FROM OUR LADY

My dear children, in these days it is so necessary to pray. I am calling you to pray the rosary with all of your heart and mind! Only I can stop what is to come! Pray the Rosary and reform your lives. Focus on my Son. Give to Him all of your heart, mind and soul. Thank God for His everlasting love. He will fill you with His grace. Thank you, my dear ones, for responding to my call.
Notes & Reflections:

FEBRUARY 23, 1990
MESSAGE FROM OUR LORD

My dear ones, as I asked My apostle, Peter, who do you say that I am, I ask you now: "Who do you say that I am? Who am I to you?" It is My heart's desire that your answer be: "Jesus, You are my heart!"

My dear ones, how I long to be your heart. How I long to love people through you. How I long to give My mercy, My understanding through you. I ask you to allow Me to be your heart so that I can take you and place you in My heart. PLEASE, DON'T RUN FROM ME. DON'T RUN FROM ME. How can I use you if you run from Me? Come, please, come back with all of your heart, and I will open your heart; and My Father and Our Spirit and I will live within your heart and, together, We will bring the lost ones home to be one again! I love you. I love you. I love you.
Notes & Reflections:

MARCH 1, 1990
MESSAGE FROM OUR LADY

My dear children, look to God for strength this Lent. Always do penance with joy. Offer everything to God. I ask of you penances, prayers, fasting and self-denial this season. Give all you have to my Son. Seek His glory, not yours.

Thank you, my dear ones, for your response to this call.

MARCH 1, 1990
MESSAGE FROM OUR LORD

My dear ones, I, your Lord, offer you life; but in order to share this life, you need to walk with Me to Calvary as I did. You will have eternal life. I invite you to follow Me in self-denial. Listen, now listen ...

(Fr. Jack's regular homily followed. In essence, he said: We must take up our cross; deny ourselves. We will be afraid, but Jesus offers His hand so we will not be alone. Our Lady wants us to know that, when we become frightened, she will help us. She will stand with us as she stood with her Son, and will hold us. Accept suffering; accept self-denial.)
Notes & Reflections:

MARCH 8, 1990
MESSAGE FROM OUR LADY

My dear children, praised be Jesus. He is your Saviour. My dear ones, pray, pray, pray. Pray and persevere. Your penance during this Lenten Season will bring great salvation to many souls. I am here with you because of the short time left for salvation. Use your time wisely. Dress my Son's wounds with your penance! I bless you, my children, and pray for you. Thank you for responding to my call.
Notes & Reflections:

MARCH 8, 1990
MESSAGE FROM OUR LADY

My dear children, **please submit continually to the will of God**. Focus on Him. Deny yourselves the affections of your pride and give totally to Him. You shall receive in return so abundantly. Strive to be good, and follow His ways. **I tell you, you are trying to control through your temper, neglect and manipulative ways.** Submit to my Son, and allow Him to be your God. You will find peace and joy in Him.

Thank you for responding to my call.
Notes & Reflections:

MARCH 8, 1990
MESSAGE FROM OUR LORD

My dear ones, My heart, this night, longs for you. If only you sought Me, alone, what I would not give you! I ask you, again, to trust in My love for you. Why do you still question? How can you question My sincere love?

Your Lord gave His life for you. How can you still say that I care nothing for you? If only you would seek Me alone and trust, there is nothing I would not grant you.

I love you, and I invite you to seek Me. It is not hard to find Me. I AM IN THE DEEPEST RECESSES OF YOUR HEART. I AM ALWAYS WITH YOU. YOU ARE NEVER ALONE!
Notes & Reflections:

MARCH 15, 1990
MESSAGE FROM OUR LORD

My little ones, as I look at you tonight, My heart opens to you. You are like little frightened children. I want you to know, dear ones, that I see the devil so active; trying to lead you astray. He is using fear to attack your heart. I invite you to come to Me, and do not be afraid. The closer you come to My heart, the more I can protect you from the devil! You have nothing to fear from Me. **Come to Me. Take My hand.** Allow Me to give you your strength, your joy. Allow Me to be your peace.

The devil has no power over you and, yet, he tries to persuade you to think he can overcome you. Denounce him, My dear ones, as I did so long ago. I love you and I will never leave you. Please, My little ones, be trusting children; not fearful children. This night I give you My joy. I ask you to accept it and let it pervade your entire being.
Notes & Reflections:

MARCH 22, 1990
MESSAGE FROM OUR LADY

My dear children, I, your Mother, come to you this night and, as your mother, I ask you to listen to what my Son, Jesus, tells you. Our Father allows Us to be with you and to invite you to always be closer to Him. I ask you, my dear ones, during the Lenten Season, when we celebrate the passion of my Son, that you devote yourself more and more to prayer. I know, my dear ones, that you feel lonely these days. Please do not think that I, your mother, abandoned you, and that my Jesus does not walk with you any longer. We are still with you. Bear the sacrifice of loneliness.

I am here this night to tell you, again, that We are always with you; always near you; always in your heart. Continue on in these days to honor my Son, responding to His grace, His call. My dear children, listen to Him speak to your heart, and allow His Spirit to fill you with peace. I love you and take you into my arms and hold you close to My heart!
Notes & Reflections:

MARCH 22, 1990
MESSAGE FROM OUR LADY

My dear children, you are my Son's little children! Seek His cross with joy. Sing to Him songs of praise. Join me as I sing joyfully to Him. He loves you. No harm shall befall you. Be like little children, and be joyful. There is peace and joy with the cross. Follow my Son and joyfully surrender to Him. Thank you for your response to my call.
Notes & Reflections:

MARCH 29, 1990
MESSAGE FROM OUR LADY

My dear children, continually pray and pray, and believe in my Son's mission! It is necessary to have faith in the mission, and trust in it with all your heart! Hope in my Son. Pray and believe in Him. Your prayers are gifts to the Father. I continually and joyfully intercede for you. Please, continually pray and have faith in the mission. Thank you, my dear ones. I bless you this night. Receive the peace of my Son.
Notes & Reflections:

MARCH 29, 1990
MESSAGE FROM OUR LORD

My dear ones, I thank you for coming this night to pray again for the salvation of the world. Your prayer touches My heart and shows Me that My passion and death were not in vain! I thank you for showing this to Me and for dressing My wounds that are still being afflicted upon Me by those who refuse My love!

I look to you this night and I see the love of My Father in your heart. I invite you to offer Me your suffering. I wish to take it from you to unite it with Mine for the salvation of all of those who are still so far from Me. I want you to know, My dear ones, what comfort your prayers give Me. Only when you are with Me forever in My Father's Kingdom, will you **fully realize the value of your prayers.** Until that time, I ask you to trust in Me, your Lord, when I tell you the value of each prayer you say with your heart.

I love you and bless you and give you this night both My Spirit of peace and mercy for your soul. I love you. I love you. I love you.
Notes & Reflections:

APRIL 5, 1990
MESSAGE FROM OUR LORD

My dear ones, **the time of My Divine Mercy is here with you!** I tell you that I am always faithful to you, even when you are unfaithful to Me! If you allow this gift of My mercy to be in your heart, then you will be faithful to Me.

I ask you this night to try harder to be faithful in your thoughts, in your words, and in your actions. As you are faithful, then My mercy will not be blocked from giving you life and to those that I send you. **This is the place of My mercy!** I call you and ask you to allow Me to give to you this night, the gift of My mercy. Accept with love and with humility this gift, and do not let your heart be troubled, for this is the time of My mercy. That is why I died for you, and that is why My Father raised Me from the dead. Be joyful and peaceful in My love!
Notes & Reflections:

APRIL 19, 1990
MESSAGE FROM OUR LADY

My dear children, believe in the Risen Christ. **Jesus is alive and dwells among you.** He is not dead, but alive! Your sufferings and pains are over. Seek peace in my Son, and peace shall be yours. When peace dwells in you, no one nor anything can disturb you. Inner peace becomes your state of being.

Seek the Risen Jesus. Always pray in faith like little children, and your prayers shall faithfully be answered. Thank you, my children, for responding to my call.
Notes & Reflections:

APRIL 19, 1990
MESSAGE FROM OUR LORD

My dear ones, I ask you not to be afraid of Me. I, your Jesus of Mercy, am here with you, and I ask you not to be afraid of Me. Why do I scare you? Why are you frightened of me? I come to love you, not to make you afraid of Me. I encourage you to touch Me in one another; to see Me in one another. Do not be afraid of Me in each other. Allow Me to touch you through your brothers and sisters. It is truly I in them and in you!

Even My disciples did not understand that with My death I banished fear. I tell you now that I have banished fear. Do not fear. Live in the hope of My love.

My dear ones, I give you life through My resurrection, and I glorify My Father. I give you My peace, and I extend to you the mercy that flows from My heart. Be My people of hope to the world, which has forgotten hope. I am coming again, but first, I want to come to the world through you.
Notes & Reflections:

APRIL 26, 1990
MESSAGE FROM OUR LADY

My dear children, come, take my hand, and I shall take you personally to my Son. My dear children, my message is one of love. Love all and show respect for one another. I wish for you to live your lives in joy and happiness. My message is simple. Love and be loved, and

peace shall be yours. My Son loves you and is with you. Live your lives in love for my Son. My blessings to you. Thank you for your response to my call.
Notes & Reflections:

MAY 3, 1990
MESSAGE FROM OUR LADY

My dear children, please respond to my call through love! Please love and accept one another for who they are. Do not reject one another. Look beyond personality and see the beauty of creation from my Son. Be grateful and rejoice in His creation. This is my wish: Please love one another. Do not reject. Thank you for responding to my call.
Notes & Reflections:

MAY 10, 1990
MESSAGE FROM OUR LADY

My dear children, please continue to love and seek my Son in your difficulties. He is your peace and your strength. Accept your difficulties with humility and joy. Trust in my Son, and He shall give you strength. Accept yourselves for who you are.

I love you, my dear ones, and intercede for you. Pray. Pray. Pray. **Prayer is the only way to peace in the world!** I bless you tonight. Thank you for your response to my call.
Notes & Reflections:

MAY 17, 1990
MESSAGE FROM OUR LADY

My dear children, please be devoted to your families. The family is the center of love where my Son dwells, for He is the center! Love your family. They are the source of His light. To love one another, you must first love your families! I love you, my dear ones, and I bestow the blessings of my Son upon you. Please be devoted to my Son through the love of your beloved ones, and you will be the shining light of my Son. Thank you, my dear ones, for your response to my call.
Notes & Reflections:

MAY 17, 1990
MESSAGE FROM OUR LORD

My dear ones, I come to you this night to remind you that you are My chosen people; the people of My heart, through whom My mercy will flow. I invite you, again, to commit yourself to loving as I love. **My dear ones, please realize that the only way to experience the joy I have for you, to it's fullest degree, is to love as I love!** Come to Me and I, your Jesus of Mercy, will again give you the strength to love. I see that you are weak. Rest in My strength, and you will experience the joy that I wish to give you.

I ask you again, listen to My words and put them into practice, so that I may touch all those through you that I call here! Live in My love and joy, true joy. My joy, given to Me by My Father, will be yours.

Notes & Reflections:

MAY 24, 1990
MESSAGE FROM OUR LADY

My dear children, on this the feast of my Son's ascension remember, as He has risen, so shall you to receive eternal glory, if you live the messages! Do not be lonely, for He has not abandoned you, but is with you. Live the messages, my dear children, and pray for peace. I bless you this night and have bestowed special graces on each one of you here this evening. Thank you for your response to my call.

Notes & Reflections:

MAY 24, 1990
MESSAGE FROM OUR LORD

My dear ones, I call you to trust Me and to trust what I have said to you as I ascended to My Father. I called upon My apostles and My disciples to trust that I would be with them always. I ask you for that same trust.

My dear ones, please listen with your heart. **Trust does not mean knowledge, it means faith.** I ask you to please believe what I said to you. It is when you don't believe, don't trust Me, that you harm yourself! If you trust, then I will be able to give you My peace and joy. Allow Me that grace, so that I may fill you with Our Holy Spirit. Give Me your heart, so that I can give you Mine!

I give you My mercy this night and I, again, commit to you My love.

Notes & Reflections:

MAY 31, 1990
MESSAGE FROM OUR LADY

My dear children, I visit you and bring tidings of joy from my Son Who loves you! As I am the mother of Him, I am also your mother, and invite you all to see His glory, as I bring Him to you.

Please, I plead with you to pray, my dear ones, and never allow Satan to molest you and distract you with invitations to temptations. I love you, my dear ones, and bless you this night. Thank you for your response to my call.

Notes & Reflections:

MAY 31, 1990
MESSAGE FROM OUR LORD

My dear ones, I hold up to you this night My mother, Mary, who is also your mother. I sent her to you because she brings Me to you as she brought Me to Elizabeth and to John. You have heard her say: "Listen to my Son." This night, My dear ones, I beg you as I say: "Listen to My mother; listen to what she says; listen to her prayer; listen to the love she has for Me and for you." I send her to you as My prophet! **SHE SPEAKS FOR ME.** Take her hand, please take her hand and allow her to lead you to Me. I tell you, My dear ones, I LOVE MY MOTHER WITH ALL OF MY HEART. PLEASE, LOVE HER WITH ALL OF YOUR HEART.
Notes & Reflections:

JUNE 7, 1990
MESSAGE FROM OUR LADY

My dear children, I am your Mother of Joy! I come to you to bring you the joy of my Son.

My dear ones, pray fervently and give thanks to my Son. Pray in reverence and be on guard against the evil one. Do not allow Satan to block your heart. Please, openly give your hearts to my Son and seek His ways by being followers of Christ. Thank you, my dear ones, for your response to my call. I bless you this night!
Notes & Reflections:

JUNE 21, 1990
MESSAGE FROM OUR LADY

My dear children, please place all your desires before my Son for His good pleasure. Please conform to His will. Restrain from the eagerness of your desires and pray! His Will **will** be done, quietly and peacefully. Pray, my dear ones, and place all your desires before my Son, conforming to His will and for His good pleasure! Thank you, my dear ones. Contemplate the goodness of my Son.
Notes & Reflections:

JUNE 28, 1990
MESSAGE FROM OUR LADY

My dear children, seek my Jesus with all of your heart. Give to Him all of your love. This, above all, is the greatest gift you could give to my Son. Love Him totally, and do not expect anything other than His love in return.

He has given you many gifts and shall continue to give to you all good things. My wish for you this night is to love my Son, your Saviour, with all of your heart! Thank you, my dear ones, for responding to my call.
Notes & Reflections:

JUNE 28, 1990
MESSAGE FROM OUR LORD

My dear ones, I ask you this evening to re-examine the motives for your prayer. I ask you to look deep within your heart to see the Holy Spirit within you. Prayer, true prayer with your heart, will lead you to obedience. **Obedience to My Father's will is your salvation and your peace.**

My dear ones, I encourage you to concentrate on the simplicity and the purity of obedience. Prayer with your hearts will lead you to that grace of obedience, and then you will truly be open in receiving the peace and joy and mercy I love to bring you from My Father. I love you and I am always with you!

Notes & Reflections:

JULY 5, 1990
MESSAGE FROM OUR LADY

My dear children, I intercede for your intentions and pray to my Jesus that you will be able to understand what a gift it is, that I have been allowed to be here with you!

Please open your hearts to my Son. I cannot give you any new messages until you live the old ones. I pray for you, and continue to ask you to be selfless and obey the will of God. I pray for your strength to change and to remain faithful to Him always. I bless you tonight, my dear ones. Thank you for your response to my call.

Notes & Reflections:

JULY 12, 1990
MESSAGE FROM OUR LORD

My dear people, I say to you again this night as I said to those in My own time: "The Reign of God is at hand." I say it now with hopeful expectations that you are listening!

I encourage you to continue on your journey of response. Share the gifts that My Father gives you with those I will bring to your life. Be My instruments of peace and of compassion and of mercy to the world.

My dear ones, it is through you that My Father's Kingdom will come and is already here! Know this; be confident in My love of you. You are strong in the strength of My Spirit. The devil wishes you to believe and to focus on your weakness, instead of leaning and focusing on the strength that I give you. **Know that you are strong.** I give you My peace, and I send My mercy upon you this night.

Notes & Reflections:

JULY 12, 1990
MESSAGE FROM OUR LADY

My dear children, there is hope in my Son. Please be strong. If you are not strong now and endure what my Son sends you, you will not be able to endure what is to come.

Have hope, and place all your trust and confidence in my Son. Pray, my children, pray! Thank you for responding to my call.
Notes & Reflections:

JULY 19, 1990
MESSAGE FROM OUR LADY

My dear children, tonight I rededicate myself to you as your **Mother of Comfort and Joy!**

I urge you to continue to pray. The sweetness of God is immeasurable. His love, peace and comfort are so overwhelming. Pray to Him, your Father. He loves you and is the Creator of life. God will bestow upon you many blessings, my dear children. He will not allow one of His children, who desires Him, to be forgotten or lost. Surrender all you have with your heart to His will in prayer. **Prayer is the key to fulfilling His will.** Thank you, my dear, dear children, for responding to my call.
Notes & Reflections:

JULY 26, 1990
MESSAGE FROM OUR LADY

My dear children, my Son is your only strength. Believe in Him. Have faith in my Son. Your life should reflect your trust in Him. Do not allow your belief to depend on the circumstances you encounter daily. Do not only believe when times are good! Trust in Him always and live in His faith daily. Believe with all of your heart, for He has allowed me to come here for you. Thank you, my dear children, for your response to my call.
Notes & Reflections:

JULY 26, 1990
MESSAGE FROM OUR LORD

My dear ones, this night I want you to begin again your appreciation of the gifts that My Father and Our Spirit give to you. How blessed you are to be living in the **time of My mercy!** Please believe and act on your belief. Live My mercy so that I can be merciful to you and to others through you. Please believe this is the time of great grace for you and for all of those who will accept it. My mercy is yours for the asking. Ask, and your heart will be filled!

My dear ones, I love you. I am here with you. My Father gives Me to you as His sign of love for you. I ask you, please accept and do not reject this gift. **This is the time of My mercy. This is the time of your salvation!**

Notes & Reflections:

AUGUST 2, 1990
MESSAGE FROM OUR LADY

My dear children, appreciate and be thankful to God for your life. God is good, and gives all good things to you. Live daily for Him. Give to Him all of your heart. I cannot tell you enough of His love for you. I cannot ask you enough to totally give your heart to Him for His good pleasure. Be thankful, my dear ones, and live for your God Who has given you life for all eternity. Thank you, my dear ones, for your response to my call.

Notes & Reflections:

AUGUST 9, 1990
MESSAGE FROM OUR LADY

My dear children, always have hope and faith in my Son. Please do not be preoccupied with the events of your day and personal thoughts. Focus totally on my Son, and you will not be distracted. This is so necessary for your spiritual growth, and is the key of life!

I love you, my dear, dear children, and bless all of you this evening. Praised be my Son, Jesus! Thank you for responding to my call.

Notes & Reflections:

AUGUST 16, 1990
MESSAGE FROM OUR LADY

My dear children, my presence here is a gift from my Son. Praised be His holy name!

Always seek my Son and live in His goodness. Have faith and trust in Him, and never cease loving Him. He will grant you eternal salvation, and peace shall be yours. Please begin to live my messages, my dear ones, for as I have told you, I cannot give you any new messages until you live the present ones! As you continue this night to celebrate the feast of my assumption, know that I celebrate my joy with you. Bless you, my dear children, and thank you for responding to my call.

Notes & Reflections:

AUGUST 23, 1990
MESSAGE FROM OUR LADY

My dear children, **my Son hears your every prayer and listens to you!** Be thankful and loving children. Always give honor to God. Focus on Him always. Give praise and glory to Him, for all good comes from Him. Do not worry about your illness. Instead, seek God in thanksgiving for your every breath. Adore Him above all. Thank you, my dear children, for responding to my call.
Notes & Reflections:

AUGUST 30, 1990
MESSAGE FROM OUR LADY

My dear children, my Son loves you deeply. Have faith in Him. Be strong during your trials, for my Son will bring you out of exile. He is devoted to you, and is all loving. Never give up hope in Him. I love you, my dear ones, and bless you this night. Praise be to God for all eternity. Thank you my dear, dear children, for responding to my call.
Notes & Reflections:

SEPTEMBER 6, 1990
MESSAGE FROM OUR LADY

My dear children, please focus all of your attention on my Son. You spend far too much energy worrying about what is to come and in preparing for that time!

My dear, dear children, please pray for peace. Pray! Pray! Pray! **Focus all your attention on my Son, and place your energy on Him.** I am your comforting mother; your loving one who listens and loves you. Pray. Please pray! Thank you, my dear ones, for responding to my call.
Notes & Reflections:

SEPTEMBER 6, 1990
MESSAGE FROM OUR LADY

My dear children, my heart is sad this night. I want you to do what I ask. I ask you to pray, and you stop praying. You offer your prayers with your lips and out of duty.

Dear children, pray with your hearts. Pray out of love. PRAY... PRAY... that is all I ask of you. Please do not stop praying! Intensify your heart's desire to pray. Your prayer is so much needed! Do I ask too much? My Son sends me to you to ask you to pray. I will pray with you if you pray from your heart. Do not give up! Do not give up! I love you. When you pray with your heart, I can remain with you... please pray.
Notes & Reflections:

SEPTEMBER 13, 1990
MESSAGE FROM OUR LORD

My dear ones, you have come to pray; you whom I have called, you who listen to Me. I am asking of you to be an example for the rest of the world. You who love Me, I ask you to be Me to the rest of the world! The way you love will not be the way people treat others, because you will be treating others as I would treat them. What I ask of you is not easy. I simply promise to be with you always. Be Me to them so that I can have mercy on them and on those who are especially so far from Me.

Thank you for daring to love as I love. Together we will again save the world.
Notes & Reflections:

SEPTEMBER 20, 1990
MESSAGE FROM OUR LADY

My dear children, in all of your struggles of life, you will find peace and joy in my Son. He loves you with a love that never changes. Whether you love Him or not, He will always love you!

Come to Him with all of your difficulties, and He will give you strength and hope. Please allow His will to be done. Thank you for responding to my call.
Notes & Reflections:

SEPTEMBER 20, 1990
MESSAGE FROM OUR LORD

My dear people, I ask you as One Who loves you with all My heart, not to be stingy with your love. **Those who love much will be forgiven much.** My love is so ineffective in this world because those, who say they follow Me, love little or selfishly in furthering their own pursuits; and they are not listening to Me.

I ask you this night to allow My love to renew your love. Love as I love, with mercy, forgiveness and compassion. My dear ones, don't you realize that, **when you judge others, you block My love?** I invite you to bring your love to Me and let Me fill you with My heart! I invite you not to be small in your loving others, for you diminish My love with that act. I give you My mercy and My healing and My peace so that you may love much! I do love you and will always love you, always!
Notes & Reflections:

SEPTEMBER 27, 1990
MESSAGE FROM OUR LADY

My dear children, as you continue to focus on my Son and pray for peace, peace will come!

Thank you for your prayers. I encourage you and urge you to continue. My Son is your hope, and blesses you with many graces. **Always thank God, and know that He does exist!** I bless you, my dear ones. Thank you for your response to my call.
Notes & Reflections:

SEPTEMBER 27, 1990
MESSAGE FROM OUR LORD

My dear ones, I am your Jesus of Mercy. This should not be confusing for you; this is the truth. This is the way I want to be with you... merciful! Time is important.

I know that you are overcome by your littleness. Sometimes you are overwhelmed by your seeming insignificance, but in My eyes you are not small or insignificant.

Because I died for you, I gave My life for you and so, My dear ones, you have infinite value! You are brought back by My death and so in the sight of the world you may be small and insignificant, but because of My dying for you, you are never small or insignificant to Me!

Allow Me to give you My mercy. I love you and, with My love and mercy, both together, they may be the salvation to the world. It will be through you that I come to them and give My mercy to them. Pray, My dear ones, that they will accept My mercy through you. I take your insignificance and draw you to Me. You belong to Me!
Notes & Reflections:

OCTOBER 4, 1990
MESSAGE FROM OUR LADY

My dear children, give praise to God and seek Him in all of your endeavors. Never give up hope. He is good and is your hope in all of your struggles.

Be at peace and accept the will of God. Do not fight Him, but love Him! You will grow in His holiness. I bless you tonight. Come, all of you, my dear children, and give thanks to God for His goodness. Thank you for your response to my call.
Notes & Reflections:

OCTOBER 4, 1990
MESSAGE FROM OUR LORD

Tonight I invite you to bear the mark of My crucifixion in your spirit. The wounds in My heart and in My hands and in My feet I bear out of love for you. I ask you in your spirit, to bear out of love for Me and the rest of the world, that which I send to you. The suffering that you live through is valuable beyond your belief and beyond your understanding for the rest of the world. I ask you in your suffering to trust Me and join your suffering to Mine so that we, together, can save the world.

My dear ones, I tell you that if you do the following and you share in My suffering, you will be in pain because the world ignores Me; and your suffering will be brief; and My Father will turn your suffering to joy and to life eternal for YOU. I love you so much that I dare to ask you to suffer with Me for the world. I am always with you. You are never alone... never!

Notes & Reflections:

OCTOBER 18, 1990
MESSAGE FROM OUR LADY

My dear children, please focus totally on my Son. He must be at the center of your life in order for you to be detached from all you are desiring. Pray and accept the journey God has planned for you. He will guide you if you let Him. Praised be my Son! He is good, and gives to you all good things. Please focus on my Son and on detachment from earthly desires which deprive your souls of spiritual growth and freshness. Thank you, my dear ones, for your response to my call.

Notes & Reflections:

OCTOBER 25, 1990
MESSAGE FROM OUR LADY

My dear children, come to my Son with all of your imperfections and weaknesses in openness. Do not hide from my Son. He is your friend, your spouse, your brother; and He loves you and will guide you if you allow Him.

Oh, my dear children, how my Son loves you. You do not have control over your desires. You are powerless without God. Open your hearts to Him and know the truth. Be faithful servants by following the word of God.

I bless you, my dear ones, as my Son blesses you. Thank you for your response to my call. Peace to you.

Notes & Reflections:

OCTOBER 25, 1990
MESSAGE FROM OUR LORD

My dear ones, I tell you this night that what you heard in the gospel is true. It is sad that following Me would cause such division in the world that My Father has created. But it is the truth; and so, I come this night to comfort you and to bathe you and your woundedness because of following Me.

I have not and will not abandon you. I thank you for your faithfulness. Please know that I know what that faithfulness is costing you. Not an ounce of your suffering goes unnoticed by Me. I take that suffering. I unite it with Mine and present it to God, Our Father, for the salvation of all My children. Continue; do not give up hope. As long as I am with you, there is reason to hope for your world!

This night I look upon you with tenderness and compassion and thanks. Receive My strength. Receive My healing for you. You are My beloved ones!
Notes & Reflections:

NOVEMBER 1, 1990
MESSAGE FROM OUR LORD

My little ones, My holy ones, you are saying "yes!" I thank you for your "yes." Through you I touch those who are in need of My mercy! You, My dear ones, are My saints.

I am with you during this time of your trial! Satan is warring against you. Lean on My strength, Do not fall into his snares. You are not alone in your struggle. I am with you.

Listen to Me. Even in your trial you are blessed. Even through your trial, if you say "yes," I will touch others with My mercy through you. I love you, My little ones, My holy, little ones. Do not be afraid. I take you to My heart!
Notes & Reflections:

NOVEMBER 8, 1990
MESSAGE FROM OUR LADY

My dear children, know you can only advance in growth at the desire of my Son. Know that change takes time! Please do not be impatient. Love my Son by being gentle on yourself. He will care for you, for He loves you. Go at His pace and be patient. He will guide you and lead you. Thank you for your response to my call.
Notes & Reflections:

NOVEMBER 8, 1990
MESSAGE FROM OUR LORD

My dear ones, I ask you, trust in Me, your Jesus of Mercy. I know your heart and I know how very many times your trust in others has been shattered.

My loved ones, I will never shatter your trust. I look into your heart. I see your fear that is there. I say to you, trust Me - I love you. I will not hurt you. I will never abandon you. I want so much to give you so very much. I can only do that if you trust Me. I see your heart. I am filled with happiness because I see how you struggle to trust.

This night I want to heal you of all those times in your life in which others have betrayed your trust in them. I want to heal you so that your trust can be restored. I want to heal you, I give you My peace, and I put My trust in you. Please put your trust in Me.
Notes & Reflections:

NOVEMBER 15, 1990
MESSAGE FROM OUR LADY

My dear children, my Son brings such joy! God is all giving and loving. He is patient and kind. He rules justly over the righteous. Open your hearts like little children, and you shall mature in the Spirit of God. Give everything to Him, and receive everything in return. Do not look back at yesterday's failings, but look at today's victory in God.

Praise be to God for all eternity. Praise Him, my little children, with dedication and commitment! Thank you for responding to my call.

Notes & Reflections:

NOVEMBER 15, 1990
MESSAGE FROM OUR LORD

My dear ones, I bring you My peace this night, and I give that gift to you as you are praying for that gift. I tell you also, that by your prayer, you have allowed My Kingdom to take root in your very selves. My Kingdom is growing within your heart, for you have given your heart to Me.

My dear ones, because you have given your heart to Me, and because My Kingdom is now growing within you, it will seem that you are out of place in this world. I see your heart, My dear ones, and I do know how uncomfortable that is for you. But know that My Kingdom is within you. That means My joy and My peace are already taking root and will soon blossom. I thank you for this suffering as of birth, as you allow my Kingdom to grow. Truly it is through you that My Kingdom will become a reality. I thank you and I love you so. I watch you grow. Nothing that you suffer for Me and My Kingdom goes unnoticed. I give you the strength of My Spirit. I give you My peace and My joy.

Notes & Reflections:

NOVEMBER 29, 1990
MESSAGE FROM OUR LADY

My dear children, blessed be my Son, Jesus!

Oh, my dear, dear children, can you not open your hearts totally to my Son, Who is wishing to give to you good tidings? Please give your control to Him. Know, my dear ones, that life must go on, and We come to grant you eternal fulfillment of eternal bliss! We come to save mankind and souls. Thank you, my dear ones, for accepting and continuing to pray for peace.

My dear children, praise be to God Who creates everything good. Please, my dear children, be good! Know that God exists, and His works are present in each of your lives. Know we have come, not to restore your earthly lives, but to save your souls and grant you eternal bliss! Know your mortal life must go on, but please do not confuse mortal life with eternal life.

Give your control to my Son. Pray for acceptance. If you live in the good works of my Son and accept His way as He molds you during your mortal life, you shall receive eternal life. Please, my dear children, accept Him and allow my Son to help you, but in the way He desires. Thank you for responding to my call.
Notes & Reflections:

NOVEMBER 29, 1990
MESSAGE FROM OUR LORD

My dear ones, I come to you this night to bring you My peace, and to say to you do not be afraid of anything. I invite you more than ever to focus on your relationship with Me. Make this the task of your life. Concentrate all of your energy on loving Me so that I can give you peace, so that I can protect you, so that I can fill you with My love, and so that I can take away your fear.

My dear ones, do not be distracted by the things that are happening. You have a place not only in My Kingdom, but in My heart. I, your Jesus of Mercy, love you. I take you to My heart. I am with you. There is nothing to fear. Pray... pray.
Notes & Reflections:

DECEMBER 6, 1990
MESSAGE FROM OUR LADY

Praised be my Son! Know, my dear, dear children, that you are like newborn babes, and I am your mother. As you celebrate the birth of my Son, know to celebrate your birth also! For as I am the mother of your Lord, I am also your mother, and have given birth to your souls!

Know also, my dear, dear children, that I shall stay here as long as my Son allows, and as long as He receives glory. So see your three years as only a new beginning, a new spiritual beginning. I bless you, my dear ones, and thank you for your prayers of acceptance. Peace to you all.
Notes & Reflections:

DECEMBER 13, 1990
MESSAGE FROM OUR LADY

My dear children, please open your hearts fully to my Son. My dear ones, please be compassionate to one another. There is still resentment and jealousy among you. Please offer this up to my Son for purification and be open to fulfill the will of God. Be loving, forgiving and compassionate.

I love you all dearly and have taken your prayers to my heart. Bless you and thank you for your continuing prayers for peace.

Notes & Reflections:

DECEMBER 20, 1990
MESSAGE FROM OUR LADY

My dear children, please unite in your love for one another, and be united in the Oneness of the Holy Trinity. Oh, my dear ones, your love and unity will be your power! You need one another.

Know that I am your mother of mercy and peace, and come to bring you joy. Know as I said "yes" to do the will of God and accepted to bear the Son of God, I also say "yes" to you and accept your prayers. I will always pray on your behalf. Please continue, my dear ones, to pray for peace.

I bless you and thank you for your response to my call.

Notes & Reflections:

DECEMBER 27, 1990
MESSAGE FROM OUR LORD

My dear ones, I am life for you. I want to give you true and eternal life. Without Me you will not truly live. Take My hands and do not be afraid any longer. I give you, this night, the strength of My life. Cling to Me and you will be strong. There will be nothing to fear as you let My life flow into you; and then, My dear ones, My life will flow through you to those I send you.

Receive My life which I have given to you and for you. You will be salvation for those who are dead in sin. You, by your example and by your love, will bring life back into them and then they will respond to My love. I thank you, I thank you. I love you and I am with you, strengthening you with the power of My life.

Notes & Reflections:

JANUARY 3, 1991
MESSAGE FROM OUR LADY

My dear children, live in the purity of God. Be good and loving children. As I am here with you this year, I ask you to be loving, forgiving and accepting of one another. I ask these three things. Please, my dear, dear children, be good and pure.

I love you, bless you and pray that you live in the fullness of God. Thank you for your response to my call.

Notes & Reflections:

JANUARY 10, 1991
MESSAGE FROM OUR LADY

My dear children, please love one another. I must continue to speak of love, for love is what is needed! Your brothers and sisters of this world are not truly bad. It is that wickedness and evil have swayed them and influenced them. They need love, not hatred or resentfulness or spite in return for their behavior towards you! Have mercy, my dear ones, and do not look for comfort from them in return for your mercy. God shall reward each of you personally and directly for the love and mercy you show to one another. He will comfort you.

Thank you, my dear ones, for your response to my call for love, which is so much needed in your world. I bless you.

Notes & Reflections:

JANUARY 17, 1991
MESSAGE FROM OUR LADY

My dear children, please do not be afraid or have fear! Unite together in the love of my Son. There is no time to panic, only time to pray and love.

You, my priests, join together; be obedient to my chosen, beloved Pope and live in the union of the Holy Trinity.

I am your Mother of Joy, and I bring to you my Son's mercy. Be loving and patient, and pray, pray, pray! You are all my beloved ones under the care of God. Have hope and trust in my Son. The will of God will be done in His glory. Thank you, my dear ones, for your response to my call.

Notes & Reflections:

JANUARY 24, 1991
MESSAGE FROM OUR LADY

My dear children, I am your **Mother of Mercy and Joy**, and you are my children begotten of God!

Please put your trust in Him and remain calm. God does exist, and I am here to tell you. You belong to Him. All those who put their trust in Him are begotten of Him. Have hope, my dear ones, my hope, and be loving. I am not disappointed in you. I simply call you to love sincerely; be honest and put your faith in Him Who has sent me. Bless you, my dear ones, and thank you for responding to my call.

Notes & Reflections:

JANUARY 31, 1991
MESSAGE FROM OUR LADY

My dear ones, I ask you to listen to me with your hearts. I have been asking this for countless generations. I, your mother, thank you for listening. My dear, dear children, I see your sorrow and I take that sorrow and present it to God, our Father, and through my Son, Jesus, our Father gives you back hope. I am with you. This is the reason for your hope.

I ask you again this night with love to pray. You and I join in prayer that the gift of hope, which my Son brings to you, will be accepted by the world. I am with you. I love you and take you to my heart. I present you this night to my Son and, We together, present you to God, Our Father. Thank you for listening. Be my hope-filled children.
Notes & Reflections:

FEBRUARY 7, 1991
MESSAGE FROM OUR LORD

My dear ones, I do not want you to be far from Me, and I, your Jesus of Mercy, am never far from you. My dear children, you are not alone. The spirit of My Father and Myself is within you. Please do not run from Me. I want to take you in My arms. I see how so often you are in pain. If you allow Me to take you, I will bring you through that pain into true love and joy. I ask you, come nearer to Me, nearer each day until you come into My heart.

My dear ones, as My heart was opened by the lance as I hung on the cross, that opening is for you. I love you and I ask you not to fear. I am here with you always. I give you peace that you need at this moment. I shed My mercy upon you, My beloved children.
Notes & Reflections:

FEBRUARY 14, 1991
MESSAGE FROM OUR LADY

My dear children, God is good, and His ever-loving hand guides you! Always put your trust in Him, and be at peace. God's plan is not what man knows, but as He knows for each one of His beloved people. Be at peace, and know that peace in His grace is surrendering openly and willingly to His will.

I bless you all, and know of your hearts' intimate suffering for my Son. Thank you, and know you are Our little, little children who will be protected and comforted. Peace to you, and thank you for your response to my call.
Notes & Reflections:

FEBRUARY 14, 1991
MESSAGE FROM OUR LORD

My dear ones, I wish to speak to you this night of My mercy for you. I wish to tell you once again My mercy is limitless. During these days I wish for you to experience My mercy by having mercy on Me. I ask you, My dear ones, to unite your suffering to Mine, to obey, to listen, and to love with My love. As you do that for each other, you will have mercy on Me.

I thank you so very much for responding. Continue in your journey. I tell you, during these days I will be very much with you, through every moment. You will never be alone. I love you -you who walk with Me the road of the cross. Be My children of mercy and of hope for your brothers and sisters.
Notes & Reflections:

FEBRUARY 21, 1991
MESSAGE FROM OUR LADY

My dear children, I love you and come as your **Mother of Peace.** Please pray for peace and for those who are at the mercy of others.

This war is one of interior and exterior turmoil. Your prayers and penance offered is soothing to God. He awaits you daily, and is your peace. Please continue to pray for peace and do penance, which is pleasing to God, for your salvation. Thank you for responding to my call.
Notes & Reflections:

FEBRUARY 21, 1991
MESSAGE FROM OUR LORD

I, your Jesus of Mercy, stand this night at the door of your heart. I ask you, My dear ones, to continue to open your hearts to Me. I am with you. Though everyone abandons you, I will be with you, and when you possess Me within your heart, you possess also My Father and Our Holy Spirit, and so you have everything.

This night I encourage you to be hope-filled. I give you My strength and My peace, and I tell you once again, which I see, you are beginning to believe. I love you, and I hold you, and I take you to My heart. As you allow Me to come into your heart, so I take you into mine. I give you this night My peace, and I command the demon of fear to leave you. **You are Mine!**
Notes & Reflections:

FEBRUARY 28, 1991
MESSAGE FROM OUR LADY

My dear children, thank you for your prayers for peace. Please continue.

Satan is the enemy who seeks to destroy all goodness and that of nature. He wishes to cause harm to you. Prayer is your protection, and God is your peace. Do not give up hope! Pray, as little ones, and know your prayers are heard.

God does exist and He is a merciful, loving and comforting God. Know He suffered to serve you and to grant you everlasting salvation. Experience your suffering, for your suffering is His suffering, the joy of living in union with Him. Peace to you, and thank you for your response to my call.
Notes & Reflections:

FEBRUARY 28, 1991
MESSAGE FROM OUR LORD

My dear ones, give me your heart. I wish to take you and give you My compassion, My comfort and My peace. I see your heart, and I see the suffering, and I see the anxiety. I tell you, I am your hope, I am the one who is the answer. You are so close to Me. **My dear mother, whom I love, brings you so close to me.** I reach out to you and I ask you to take My hand - feel the hope and the mercy. I tell you again this night, I am with you. You are not alone. My adversary wishes you to think you are abandoned. I take you to My heart and hold you there. If you feel suffering, it is truly the suffering of My own heart. I love you, I love you!
Notes & Reflections:

MARCH 14, 1991
MESSAGE FROM OUR LADY

My dear children, please see this Lenten season as a great blessing from God. He is all good, and your suffering is a blessing unified in His goodness. Satan is trying very hard to disrupt your peace, but know your faith in trusting my Son will bring you great consolation. I bless you all tonight, my dear little ones, and ask you to continue in your walk with my Son. Thank you for responding to my call.
Notes & Reflections:

MARCH 14, 1991
MESSAGE FROM OUR LORD

My dear people, My dear ones, I ask you this night to turn again to the road of mercy. You have not been merciful. I ask you to strive not to judge. I see your heart, and I see that you are trying, but I also see how easy it is for you to allow your heart to grow cold and to become hardened. My dear ones, I want to take you in My arms. When you are not merciful, you prevent me from embracing you as I wish. Each of you is My disciple of mercy. I love you. I ask you not to give up. **I do not give up on you!**
Notes & Reflections:

MARCH 21 ,1991
MESSAGE FROM OUR LADY

My dear children, as you enter into passion week, seek the passion of my Jesus. Contemplate His suffering and turmoil, and visualize His blood which was shed for you. In contemplating His suffering, you shall see the good which He gave to the world through His redemptive suffering. This, in turn, shall purify you.

Oh, praised be my Son, your Lord. Bless you my dear ones, this night; and thank you for your response to my call.
Notes & Reflections:

APRIL 4, 1991
MESSAGE FROM OUR LADY

My dear children, always look to your Risen Lord for your joy. Know that His suffering was in order for you to obtain the true and everlasting joy and bliss of eternal happiness! Always choose God and be open to His way, as He molds you and leads you on the straight path, the only path, His path to His Kingdom.

Rejoice in my Son; and bless you all, my dear children, tonight and always. Thank you again for your commitment to responding to my call.
Notes & Reflections:

APRIL 4, 1991
MESSAGE FROM OUR LORD

My dear ones, I your Jesus, come to you this night to give you, as I gave My disciples long ago, My peace. You are My disciples now! I see, My dear ones, how you run after many things. I tell you this night accept My peace. Accept My quiet so that I may give you My joy. Believe Me when I say you share now in My resurrection, if you would only open your hearts to that gift. I love you! I invite you again to truly accept My love so that your anxiety, fear and worry may be quieted.

This, My dear ones, is the time of refreshment for you, time that My mercy can be so evident if you allow it to be. I, **your Risen Lord**, am with you. My mother is likewise with you. Allow her to take your heart to bring you closer to My heavenly Father.
Notes & Reflections:

APRIL 11, 1991
MESSAGE FROM OUR LADY

My dear children, pray, pray, pray! Never cease praying. Please pray for my beloved priests and remain obedient to the Church. Thank you, my dear ones. Grow and be happy little

children in the loving arms of God. Bless you and thank you for responding to my call.
Notes & Reflections:

APRIL 11, 1991
MESSAGE FROM OUR LORD

My dear ones, I come to you this night to speak but one word, and that word is LOVE. I have shown you, through My passion and death, of My love for you. My Father, Our Father, has shown His love for Me by raising Me from the dead. This word, LOVE, is truly the sign that you are My disciples. I invite you again this night to love, to love as best you can, to love with your heart. This love will cut through all prejudice, all judgment. **This love is MY LOVE.**

My dear ones, as I looked down from My cross, down to My mother, and through her, down through all the ages, I saw that My act of love and death can be your love. I bless you this night with My love. My love is the love of My Father and Our Spirit. That love is your life.
Notes & Reflections:

APRIL 18, 1991
MESSAGE FROM OUR LADY

My dear children, God remains faithful to your friendship. Turn to Him always. Be happy little children and go to Him. He will care for you. Be obedient and disciplined little children, so that you may grow in truth and in His purity.

I bless you, my children, as my Son blesses you. Seek Him always. **Praised be Jesus**. I love you and thank you for your continual prayers for peace.
Notes & Reflections:

APRIL 18, 1991
MESSAGE FROM OUR LORD

My dear faithful ones, I thank you for your perseverance. I look this night into your hearts and I see Our Holy Spirit - the Spirit of Love. I come this night to encourage you, to be with you always.

I do give you My flesh and blood as your nourishment in each Eucharist. I see, My dear ones, how devoted you are to Me in My Eucharist. I want you to know how pleasing this is to My Father. I want you to know how many souls come to Me because of your love for the Eucharist.

I thank you and I bestow upon you this night the strength of healing that you need. I, this night, your Lord, your Jesus of Mercy, cast out the fear that is there, and give you My peace. Fear not, dear little ones, **I love you!**
Notes & Reflections:

APRIL 25, 1991
MESSAGE FROM OUR LADY

My dear children, be the little children of God and grow into His discipleship! I tell you, my dear ones, that many followed my Son, as His disciples; and then turned and walked away because they could not accept His truth, because of their human ways and skepticism.

I ask you to follow Him in His truth. His truth is the only way. Please pray and be loving, merciful, kind and compassionate. Do not allow your human ways to persuade you from being His disciple through your skepticism. Believe in God and show your love for Him through your love for others. Begin living His love and speaking kindly of His love. Bless you and thank you for your response to my call.

Notes & Reflections:

MAY 9, 1991
MESSAGE FROM OUR LADY

My dear children, you are my children of joy, the little joyful children of God. My dear ones, as I present you to my Son, I ask you to turn to Him. He is the only way. Please, my dear ones, be good and show your goodness through your actions. **Give glory and praise to my Son through your actions**. The evil one is trying so desperately to persuade you otherwise.

Endure all with patience and trust in my Son. His will will be done, and His protection is on all who seek Him in honesty. Pray to the Spirit, my comforter, and never give up hope. I bless you this night, my dear little children. Know God knows each one of you. Please love Him always. Thank you for responding to my call.

Notes & Reflections:

MAY 9, 1991
MESSAGE FROM OUR LORD

My dear ones, I call you to be My disciples of hope to this world. If you accept this call, I will be able to touch so many through you. You will be children of hope, bright shining lights for all to see. You have nothing to fear any longer. You will be hope for the world, My hope, the hope of the Spirit. As I ascended to My Father, I promised to send Our Spirit. The Holy Spirit is with you now. That is why you are hope-filled. Spread that sign of My love to all. Thank you. I love you, and I give you this night, if you will accept it, the gift of hope.

Notes & Reflections:

MAY 16, 1991
MESSAGE FROM OUR LADY

My dear children, you are my children of God. My dear ones, as I present you to my Son, I ask you to turn to Him. He is the only way. Please, my dear ones, be good and show your goodness through your actions. Give glory and praise to my Son through your actions. The evil one is trying so desperately to persuade you otherwise. Endure all with patience and trust in my Son. His will will be done and His protection is on all who seek Him in honesty. Pray to the Spirit, my comforter, and never give up hope.

I bless you this night, my dear little children. Know God knows each one of you. Please love Him always. Thank you for responding to my call.

Notes & Reflections:

MAY 16, 1991
MESSAGE FROM OUR LORD

My dear ones, I come to you this night to tell you that I stand before My Father and your Father to intercede for you, and My Father and your Father send Our Spirit to you. This night, my dear one; it is the Spirit of courage. Do not be faint of heart in living as I invite you to live. Be courageous in your daily actions. Live the love that I give. There is no need at all for you to be faint of heart or timid. You have the gift of Our Spirit within you. Allow that Spirit, my dear ones, to guide you, to protect you, and to touch all of those who come to you. Believe me when I say to you, **it is through you that I, your Jesus, touch this world**. Have courage, my little ones. You bring great joy to My mother.

Notes & Reflections:

MAY 23, 1991
MESSAGE FROM OUR LADY

My dear ones, never lose sight of God. Always place your heart into his loving arms. At all cost be faithful, loving and loyal to Him. Make your attitude that of my Son's by following Him and imitating His ways the best way you can. Love Him always no matter what happens personally in your life, for He is your life, and He is life.

I bless you tonight, my dear little children. Please be loving and love my Son always. Thank you for responding to my call. Peace to you.

Notes & Reflections:

MAY 30, 1991
MESSAGE FROM OUR LORD

My dear ones, I tell you, I do listen to your prayer. I ask you tonight to listen to My prayer, My request of you. I ask you, **give to Me your heart so that I can offer your heart to My heavenly Father**. Give to Me all of those things which worry you and cause you fear. I will take them and give to you My peace.

My dear ones, I love you and I ask that you love from your heart, all of those I send to you. I tell you tonight that I take you into My arms. You are the children of God. Peace and mercy flow to you and through you.

Notes & Reflections:

JUNE 6, 1991
MESSAGE FROM OUR LADY

My dear children, I, your Mother of Joy, ask you to come to me with open hearts and open arms into my mantle. I will not deny any who do not deny my Son. How can I deny your requests when you, with openness, do not deny my Son. I, in turn, will go to my Son. He will not deny me, for I do not deny Him.

Please, my dear ones, know God does exist. This is reality and I have been sent to tell you. Please pray and live in the purity of God according to the doctrine of the Church governed by my beloved Pope. Bless you my dear ones. I have taken your prayers into my Immaculate Heart. There your prayers will turn to the purity of God. Thank you for your response to my call.

Notes & Reflections:

JUNE 6, 1991
MESSAGE FROM OUR LORD

My dear ones, I say to you this night, as I said long ago, **the first commandment is to honor God, My Father and your Father, with all of your heart, with all of your being**. My dear ones, allow Me, your Jesus, to be at the center of your heart. My mother and I, through the Holy Spirit, have shown you how your life goes when you allow Me to be in the center.

I ask you again, **allow Me to be the center of your life**. I will then be able to give you all that you need. This night I invite you to recommit your heart to Me.

Notes & Reflections:

JUNE 20, 1991
MESSAGE FROM OUR LADY

My dear ones, I, your mother, ask you to be committed to God in loyalty to Him. Please pray, pray! I must tell you that loyalty to God leads to depending on Him, and freedom. Pray whether you desire to or not. Be committed to Him as your first priority. I bless you all, my dear ones, and thank you for responding to my call.

Notes & Reflections:

JUNE 20, 1991
MESSAGE FROM OUR LORD

My dear ones, My Father knows what you need. You need Me, your Jesus of Mercy. My Father knows that you need encouragement and so this night, My dear ones, I am here to encourage you in your journey. This night I give you My strength to persevere. I see the many difficulties. I want you to know that I am with you during every moment. There is nothing that you suffer that I don't suffer with you. I love you. This gift of My love is enough for you. Believe with all of your heart that you are in possession of My love. I take you this night to God, My Father. Be encouraged little ones. You are living in the Kingdom of My love.

Notes & Reflections:

JUNE 27, 1991
MESSAGE FROM OUR LADY

My dear children, please keep your eyes focused on my Son. Never lose sight of Him. He is your light to lead you through the narrow gate which only He can bring you through. Please, my dear ones, pray in contemplation of what is good. Pray peacefully and await the will of God, peacefully and with patience. Do not run ahead and expect answers at your call. Be righteous in Him and you will be safe. Your answers will be done according to the will of God, at His glory, which will result in your happiness. Thank you, my dear children, for responding to my call.

Notes & Reflections:

JULY 4, 1991
MESSAGE FROM OUR LADY

My dear children of the Americas, I, your Mother of Joy, come to bless you with my peace and the peaceful blessings of my Son. On this day, know your independence is one of freedom for prayer and doing the righteousness of God. I, your mother of this nation whose God is your Lord, bring peace and many graces of blessings. Pray, my dear little children, for all the world whose independence is in jeopardy. Never cease praying for peace; for peace and freedom belong to all the world not just your country in which you live. I bless you my dear ones. Thank you for responding to my call.

Notes & Reflections:

JULY 4, 1991
MESSAGE FROM OUR LORD

My dear ones, I, your Lord, give words of peace to you, not only from My lips, but from My heart and from My actions for you. I am with you this night, here in the United States, and My heart is heavy because you celebrate your independence from Me. You, as a nation, are killing yourself with your independence from Me. I, your Lord and Saviour, beg you this night to renounce that independence and to make this day a new beginning of declaration of your dependence upon My Sacred Heart.

My children, only in this dependence will you experience true freedom. As you depend upon Me, then I can break those chains which bind your heart. I can give you joy and peace which you, in your independence, will never take. Hear me! Listen! I invite you - FOLLOW ME. I WILL BRING YOU LIFE.

Notes & Reflections:

JULY 11, 1991
MESSAGE FROM OUR LORD

My dearest ones, I, your Jesus of Mercy, encourage you this night to give to those whom I send into your life the gifts that I have given to you and that I give you again from My heart this night; the gift of My compassion, the gift of My joy, the gift of My love, the gift of My peace, the gift of My mercy, the gift of Our Holy Spirit.

All of these, My dear ones, I have given freely to you because I love you. As you love Me, give those same gifts to all those that I send into your life. Love them with My love. Embrace them with the gentleness of My heart and know, My dear ones, that as you do this I am with you. I love you. You are mine. You are never alone.

Notes & Reflections:

JULY 18, 1991
MESSAGE FROM OUR LORD

My dear ones, how long, how long do I have to say to you that I come to comfort and to be merciful to you? You still hesitate! Please believe that My will for you is your eternal joy with Me. I am with you. Please allow Me to be truly with you. Again, this night, I invite you to give Me your heart. I so want to take care of you. Please do not prevent Me, by your pride and your fear, from taking care of you. I say to you - follow Me, allow My life to be yours. I want to be one with you.

I give you this night My mercy, My love, and My peace. Please accept these gifts from Me, from My Sacred Heart to your heart, made sacred by My love.

Notes & Reflections:

JULY 25, 1991
MESSAGE FROM OUR LADY

My dear children, I, your Mother of Joy, come to plead with you to love. My dear children, you must be like little children in your love for one another. There is far too much hatred among men. I ask you to love one another unconditionally. So not only listen, but hear. Please, my dear ones, it is only love that will save. Love is the greatest virtue. I continue to thank God for allowing me to come here to be with you. Please now be grateful to my Son who loves you and graces you. Please, please, love one another. Thank you for responding to this call of my Son.

Notes & Reflections:

JULY 25, 1991
MESSAGE FROM OUR LORD

My dear ones, I come to you this night to tell you again that you are never alone, that I am with you. I AM ALWAYS WITH YOU! I see, my dear ones, how discouraged you become in your weakness. I, Your Lord, tell you that I am not saddened by your weakness. I am saddened by your sin. I can take you in your weakness, but I cannot take you in your sin, because you turn from Me. Please do not turn from Me. Turn to Me in your weakness so that I can comfort you. Your sin keeps you from Me in your weakness. Be embarrassed by your sin, not by your weakness. Realize, my dear ones, that I, your Lord, love you. Come to Me in your weakness. I will heal you. Do not be overburdened. I will carry your burden. I give you My strength. I give you My love. If you accept these gifts, you will not be overcome by your weakness, and your sin will be washed away. I AM WITH YOU!

Notes & Reflections:

AUGUST 1, 1991
MESSAGE FROM OUR LADY

My dear children, I can only ask you to love unconditionally, because my love for my Son is unconditional, and my hope is that you all hasten to His call. My dear little children, God loves you and only brings good tidings to you. He wishes to cleanse you with His truth and holiness. Be open to His call and do your best everyday to follow the only way, the way of my Son.

Bless you, my dear little ones. I bless you and wrap you in my mantle of prayer. Thank you for responding to my call of love.
Notes & Reflections:

AUGUST 1, 1991
MESSAGE FROM OUR LORD

My dear ones, this is the time of My mercy. I see your hearts and the hearts of all people. And I see the good as well as the evil - so little good, so much evil. But I give you My hope because the good, little though it be, can be the yeast to bring about much good, to bring about conversion of those who are steeped now in evil. That is why this is the time of My mercy. Take advantage of this time. I love you, My dear ones, for presenting your hearts to Me. I ask you again this night to pray with all of your might and with all of your heart for those who are most in need of My mercy, those who are gone from My heart. I give you My peace and My hope. I take you this night to My heart. I LOVE YOU!
Notes & Reflections:

AUGUST 8, 1991
MESSAGE FROM OUR LADY

My dear children, I am your Mother of Grace who possesses all goodness from my Son. He wishes for you to live in His Oneness of the Holy Trinity. Please, my dear children, do not delay in loving. There is little time to put aside love for your brethren. Turn to my Son and He shall bestow on you the many graces of eternal life. Live in peace. Remember, without love there cannot be peace. LOVE, LOVE, LOVE my Son by loving one another. Praise be my Son. Bless you, my children, and thank you for responding to my call.
Notes & Reflections:

AUGUST 8, 1991
MESSAGE FROM OUR LORD

My dear ones, I ask you this night to trust Me. You say that I am your Lord. If I am, then trust Me. My dear ones, I see in your heart; and I see so much confusion, trying to understand My plan, the plan of My heavenly Father. Please, My dear ones, don't try to understand; either I am your Lord or I am not. If I am, then trust that I will lead you and I will take care of you. I know, My loved ones, that many times this is so difficult for you to do. In those times especially, I am with you and My dear mother is with you. Use her as an example, as THE EXAMPLE of trust in God's will and in God's plan. How could I say that I love you if I were not ready to take care of you. Allow Me to be your Lord. You do this when you trust Me. This night, I give you strength to trust; and I give you hope beyond this world's hope, and I give you My peace.
Notes & Reflections:

AUGUST 22, 1991
MESSAGE FROM OUR LADY
(FEAST OF THE QUEENSHIP OF THE BLESSED MOTHER)

My dear children, I, your Mother of Joy, come to invite you again to be little children of God. God does exist, my dear ones. Please be pure, have faith and trust in my Son. Fidelity to God will keep your hearts pure, and simpleness is the way. Seek always to please God by seeking to do His will.

I bless you, my dear little, little children - my children whom I bring to my Son. He shall grace you abundantly. Keep your eyes fixed on Him in a true intimacy which He is seeking from you. Bless you, my dear ones, and thank you for your response to my call.
Notes & Reflections:

AUGUST 22, 1991
MESSAGE FROM OUR LORD

My dear ones, I, your Jesus of Mercy, tell you this night that My mother is the queen of My heart, because it was from her heart that Our Holy Spirit formed My heart. My dear ones, as you honor her, you honor Me, and you give glory to Our Father. Words, human words, cannot even begin to phrase the love that I have for her. She is MY MOTHER. I love her. I ask you to love her also. She so much wants you as her dearest children. She tells God Our Father that she sees Me in all of you. That is how much she loves you. Love her, run to her before you are lost. Again this night, my dear ones, I give you My mother. Cherish her as I cherish her, and she will lead you not only to Me but to God Our Father. Peace, My dear ones, peace to you.
Notes & Reflections:

AUGUST 29, 1991
MESSAGE FROM OUR LADY

My dear children, I come to you because the grace of my Son has allowed His goodness to be shed upon all mankind. He desires you to be filled with His eternal blissful spirit and share in eternal happiness. Please, my dear children, unite in harmony and live peacefully. Allow your behavior to speak for the words of your action. Be loving and live in my Son's goodness. There is no time to shed wasteful energy when God has granted you the gift of love. Please be my little children through love as He loves you. I bless you, my dear ones, and invite you once again to be committed to my Son in love. Thank you for responding to my call.

Notes & Reflections:

SEPTEMBER 5, 1991
MESSAGE FROM OUR LADY

My dear children, the graces of my Son do not present pressure. There is only peace with my Son. Be at peace and be calm in Him. Look to Him for comfort and follow the truth in unity. Please, my dear little children, God is good. Come to my Son like little children, childlike, joyful and carefree. Thank Him. How grateful and happy I am that He has allowed me the grace to be here with you. I bless you, my dear little children, and bring you my Son's peace. Thank you for responding to my call.

Notes & Reflections:

SEPTEMBER 5, 1991
MESSAGE FROM OUR LORD

My dear ones, I am your Jesus of Mercy, and yet you still don't believe this. You still look at your sinfulness. My dear ones, don't you realize that you will always be sinful until you give your heart completely to Me? You hide from Me your sin. Please give Me your sin. I took that sin upon Myself on the cross; I, your Lord, who takes away your sin. Please do not hold fast to it and do not hide from Me because - don't you see that My love overcomes everything? You are weighted down in this sinfulness. Allow Me this once, this night, to take your sin, to heal your heart. I give you my peace. You are overcome by your sin. Sin can never overcome me. I LOVE YOU.

Notes & Reflections:

SEPTEMBER 12, 1991
MESSAGE FROM OUR LADY

My dear children, live in simpleness, simple ways and loving ways. Always seek to be calm, taking day by day. Oh, my children of God, blessed are you who follow in simpleness. Seek purity and live good, not bad ways. I bless you this evening with the grace from God. Strive to be simple. My message is to love and be simple. Do not try to understand, simply live day by day in my Son's light. Thank you for responding to my call.

Notes & Reflections:

SEPTEMBER 12, 1991
MESSAGE FROM OUR LORD

My dear ones, as I call you to follow Me, I see so often your trying to understand. My dear ones, what I say to you now, what I said to those when I was walking here with them here on earth does not always make sense to your human mind and understanding. I invite you this night, once again, to trust Me, your Lord and Saviour. I do have words of everlasting life for you, and what I ask of you does not make sense to the world. What I ask of you makes sense only when you listen with your heart through My Spirit which is in you; I say to you this night - I give you My peace to calm your mind. I invite you to obedience and to trust. They will lead you into My heart. I LOVE YOU, I LOVE YOU, AND I AM WITH YOU ALWAYS.

Notes & Reflections:

SEPTEMBER 19, 1991
MESSAGE FROM OUR LADY

My dear children, praise be my Son. My dear ones, please seek intimacy with my Son. He loves because He is love. He loves you and calls you to His mystical love. Oh, my dear ones, Satan is desperately trying to present you temptations and confusion. Know that as you focus on my Son that your temptations can only be short lived. Always seek God and live in His goodness like little children, and you shall be protected. I bless you with the grace of God, and I thank you for responding to my call.

Notes & Reflections:

SEPTEMBER 19, 1991
MESSAGE FROM OUR LORD

My dear ones, I love you. This night I look into your hearts and I see the desire that you have there to love and to serve My heavenly Father. I also see how often you become discouraged by your lack of love and your lack of response. Please, my dear ones, I invite you to give Me this night even the little love that you have in your heart, and I will make that little love grow. Do not be discouraged, your journey is not over yet. I am with you to encourage you, to protect you and to love you. Come with your doubt, come with your worry, come with your little love into my arms and rest, and love. You are mine! I bless you and heal you of your lack of love. Please accept this healing from me this night.

Notes & Reflections:

OCTOBER 3, 1991
MESSAGE FROM OUR LADY

My dear children, peace to you and praise to God. Oh my dear children, take time to absorb the love of my Son. Take time to allow Him to dwell in your being, bringing you His fruits of grace. Please my dear ones, oh how loving He is and how He wishes you His tranquility of peace. Allow yourselves to be loved by one another. Allow others to take care of you with their loving ways, and please allow my Son to love you and dwell peacefully. Thank you, my dear ones for responding to my call of peace and love within your lives.

Notes & Reflections:

OCTOBER 10, 1991
MESSAGE FROM OUR LORD

My dear ones, I give to you this night because you asked Me to be here. You invite Me with your heart. My heavenly Father sent Me to you again. My dear ones, this night I make a request to you with your love to show other people how much I, your Jesus of Mercy, want to be with them also. Show them that My being with you here is not exclusive, but because you have invited Me. Please, my dear ones, help them to see by your joy and your love that My being with them is as simple as their inviting Me to be with them. It is the desire of My heart.

I love you. I thank you for inviting Me in. I will always be with you. You are not alone. Please show others that they do not have to be alone either. I long to take all of My children into My embrace, and to My heart. You are the ones who can help Me. For this purpose, I bless you this night again with My joy, and My peace, and My mercy. Bring those again to all whom you meet.

Notes & Reflections:

OCTOBER 17, 1991
MESSAGE FROM OUR LADY

My dear children, I ask you this night to rededicate yourselves to my Immaculate Heart and to my Son's most Sacred Heart. You, my little ones, shall be put to the test. It is through your daily struggles that you grow. Pray with renewed vigor. Please pray, pray, pray. It brings me great joy to see you gathered to pray. I bless you and thank you for your response to my call.

Notes & Reflections:

OCTOBER 17, 1991
MESSAGE FROM OUR LORD

My dear ones, I come to you this night to say plainly I am never separated from My cross. My Father raised Me from the dead and yet, My dear ones, I still bear the wounds of My crucifixion. Just as I, in that way, am never separated from My cross, so are you never separated from yours. Dear ones, please listen - do not try to separate Me from My cross. Do not try to separate yourself from your cross. Together we continue to save the world. My wounds, My dear ones, are now glorified. I, this night, glorify your wounds through mine. Your woundedness is not defeat but hope, encouragement and life for this world. I embrace you as you embrace your cross. I give you strength and courage to continue to bear it.

I bless you this night again with the mercy that comes through My wounds from My cross. I invite you, in turn, to shed that same mercy through your woundedness from your cross to others. I AM ALWAYS WITH YOU!

Notes & Reflections:

OCTOBER 24, 1991
MESSAGE FROM OUR LORD

My dear ones, I am here this night with you to bestow upon you, each of you, My healing mercy. Open your heart to receive this gift. This is the gift that will truly heal you for eternity. This is the gift that I bought for each of you on the cross. This is the gift that will bring you from where you are to Me. Allow this gift to wrap you in My love. As you receive My Mercy, as you allow it to heal you, you will begin to see what really matters.

I tell you, My dear ones, you are still concerned with the wrong things. Allow My mercy to calm you, to relieve your anxiety, and to restore the joy that My Father has placed within you from the very moment of your conception. As a reminder of that joy, I continue to give you My mother. I love you. I love you.

Notes & Reflections:

OCTOBER 31, 1991
MESSAGE FROM OUR LADY

My dear children, praised be my Son. My dear little ones, never give up hope in my Son. Be strong in your faith. Put on your shield of armor. Never lose focus of your Jesus, your God. The evil one is desperately trying to ruin your happiness through despair. Satan is trying to interrupt my plan, but he cannot because God exists, and God is with me. Focus on my Son. The war is a war against God. Live in simpleness and never lose sight of the truth. Pray, pray, and live in simpleness. Bless you, my dear little children, and thank you for responding to my call.

Notes & Reflections:

OCTOBER 31, 1991
MESSAGE FROM OUR LORD

My dear ones, I am with you this night to encourage you on your way of holiness. I look at your heart and at everything else. I see that spark of My Holy Spirit and the Spirit of My Father. I encourage you, My dear ones, fan that spark into a flame to be My holy ones, My lights to this world. My affection and my love for you is limitless. I ask you to begin to realize how much I, your Lord, depend upon you in your holiness to touch those to whom I send you. My dear ones, it is I who touch them, it is I... If you were to ask me for one thing this night, I encourage you to ask for holiness. This is the gift that I give. You are My holy ones - be joyful with this gift, and know that I AM ALWAYS WITH YOU!

Notes & Reflections:

NOVEMBER 7, 1991
MESSAGE FROM OUR LADY

My dear children, pray, pray, love. Please strive to restore love, mercy, compassion, respect, dignity and honesty, as my Son has asked.

Notes & Reflections:

NOVEMBER 7, 1991
MESSAGE FROM OUR LORD

My dear ones, you belong to Me. I have come to you to find My lost ones. Many of you were lost, but you chose to begin to listen to My love and now you are found. I come this night to give you courage to realize you are Mine, and to ask you to find my lost ones. Find them by your mercy; find them by your love and compassion. They will be attracted to you as lead is to a magnet because they do not want to be lost, but they are so very lost. I give you again this night the love of My heart. My dear ones, you were lost and now you are home. This gift is there for all to receive. Through you, it is being offered again to all. I thank you, I love you. I am with you to bring the lost ones home!

Notes & Reflections:

NOVEMBER 14, 1991
MESSAGE FROM OUR LADY

Please unite in the graces of my Son. Know the evil one is attempting to destroy the love of mankind. Be children of God and do not lose your focus on God. He is your protection. He gives you life. Fight as soldiers of God for God. Begin now, my dear ones, to put your armor of love on. Be prepared for the battle is against God. Pray, pray, pray.

Notes & Reflections:

NOVEMBER 14, 1991
MESSAGE FROM OUR LORD

My dear ones, I am here with you this night to speak again not to your mind but to your heart. So many reject My love, and My mercy, and My forgiveness. When they reject those gifts, then they reject My reign in their hearts. They continue to search, but they will never find Me because they look in the wrong place and do the wrong thing.

My dear ones, as I look into your hearts this night, I want to tell you again that My Kingdom is already in you. When you accept My mercy, when you accept My love, when you accept My forgiveness, you experience My reign over you. Live now in My Kingdom so that you can live fully when My Kingdom is complete. I give you this night the strength to open your heart and to allow more and more of My Kingdom to surround you. Know that you who are living in My Kingdom will be the example to those I send you. I love you. You fill Me with joy this night and so I fill you with My joy this night.

Notes & Reflections:

NOVEMBER 21, 1991
MESSAGE FROM OUR LADY

My dear children, live by the way of humility, love, silence and discernment. Be prudent and always focus on my Son. He is not in a far away place. He is here, my dear children. Be the little children of God and hope in my Son. Please, please, pray for peace of mankind. Your humanity is now in danger. I bless you, my dear ones. Thank you for responding to my call.

Notes & Reflections:

DECEMBER 5, 1991
MESSAGE FROM OUR LADY

My dear children, I, your mother, come in sorrow; sorrow for mankind's lack of love. My dear ones, as my Son's mercy pours out into this world, my sorrow is for those lost souls who choose to walk away from Him; and it pierces my Immaculate Heart. Oh, how my Son still bears the wounds of humanity for your salvation. Please, my dear ones, pray and love. Your

prayer finds a gracious hearing with my Son. Love. Your love dresses my Son's wounds Who loves you and desires your love. Thank you, my dear ones, for responding to my call in these days of sorrow.
Notes & Reflections:

DECEMBER 5, 1991
MESSAGE FROM OUR LORD

I come this night to thank you for putting My words into practice, for responding to the invitation that My mother has given to you. This night, my dear ones, My heart overflows with joy and with sadness; with joy because of you. Do you not realize that the very gift of prayer is a grace from My heavenly Father to you? That very grace of prayer is offered to each one. That is why I say this night My heart is overflowing with joy and with sorrow; with joy because you accept this grace, this very grace of prayer for this world; in sorrow because so many still choose not to accept this grace, choose not to follow and put into practice My words, choose not only not to accept My mother's invitation, but to mock her. Do they not know when they mock her, they mock Me? She is My heart. Thank you for loving her so much. When you love her, you love Me. My dear ones, this night I give you My peace and the gratitude of your Jesus. I thank you. I love you. I AM WITH YOU ALWAYS!
Notes & Reflections:

DECEMBER 12, 1991
MESSAGE FROM OUR LADY

My dear children, I, your mother of joy, celebrate your years of prayer. Please, my dear little children, continue your prayers. The blessings of God are upon you. Look to Him for joy, peace, hope, truth, mercy and humility. I thank you, my dear beloved ones, for your prayers which this world is in so much need. Bless you, and please continue. I shall be here because my Son is here and He loves you. Prepare for my festival in thanksgiving to God for allowing me to be here since December 19, 1989. Thank you for responding to my call.
Notes & Reflections:

DECEMBER 12, 1991
MESSAGE FROM OUR LORD

My dear ones, I come to you this night to say to you how blessed are you among all people. How blessed are you for you have My mother who is always with you, not only because she obeys the Father's command, but because she also wishes to be with you. She loves you so. My dear ones, thank you for loving her, thank you for loving her. When you love her, you love Me, yourself. We have blessed you with her presence. Thank you for accepting this blessing for it will not go away. It will last until I come. I give you My peace and My mercy.
Notes & Reflections:

DECEMBER 19, 1991
MESSAGE FROM OUR LADY

My dear children, I give to you the rose of my heart which is the rose of my Son, His heart. Oh, my dear little children, do not despair but rejoice in my Son, your Saviour. Pray always for peace. Peace shall come if you are committed to love and compassion for a peaceful humanity. Your prayers can mitigate what is coming according to God, so form together in unity and pray, pray, pray!

In thanksgiving, I thank God for His loving kindness, love and goodness He extends to you to allow me to be here with you. I shall continue to be here because of your generosity and love to one another. Thank you, my dear ones, for allowing this to be the center of my Son's divine mercy. I bless you and thank you for your response to my call.
Notes & Reflections:

DECEMBER 19, 1991
MESSAGE FROM OUR LORD

My dear ones, I ask you again tonight to trust in God. My Father sends Me to you to ask you to trust. Those things which so often cause you anxiety, those things which so often trouble your heart, those are the things in which you do not trust God. I remind you, My dear ones, that nothing is impossible to My Father, or to Me. I encourage you to live your life to give honor to My Father; and, when you are tempted to fear, know that I am with you. I encourage you to take My hand. I will never let go of you. You are in My heart. I love you. Just, believe, have courage. I give you this night My peace. Allow this gift, My dear ones, to surround your very souls.
Notes & Reflections:

JANUARY 9, 1992
MESSAGE FROM OUR LADY

My dear children, I come to you because of the goodness of my Son who has allowed me to be here with you. He is here with you, my dear ones, and His divine mercy flows out unto you. My dear ones, please unite. Please be peaceful with one another and loving. Pray, pray, pray, my little children. Reflect His love in your actions and words. My dear ones, this is the age of my Son's mercy. Please allow His love and mercy to dwell in you through openness. Focus on Him and He will guide you in love. Thank you, my dear ones, for responding to my call.
Notes & Reflections:

JANUARY 16, 1992
MESSAGE FROM OUR LADY

My dear children, peace to you always. My dear little ones, please pray and let the goodness of God never leave you, that you will always remain obedient and loving little children. Please, my children, focus on my Son. Trust in Him; trust, trust, trust. Do not judge one another harshly. Always seek to please God by loving one another. Be cautious that you may hurt someone because of lack of humility. Love through trusting and obedience to God. I bless you, my dear ones. Please be cautious of your hidden pride. Place my Son first always. He is the only one to give you comfort, joy and peace. Thank you for responding to my call.

Notes & Reflections:

JANUARY 16, 1992
MESSAGE FROM OUR LORD

My dear ones, I come to you this night to tell you again I love you, and to invite you again to acceptance - the acceptance of My Father's will for you. My dear ones, only in that acceptance of His will comes the peace for which you seek and the joy that your soul is so much in need of. They go hand-in-hand. Many times you believe that if you accept My Father's will, that will bring pain and suffering to you. I present to you this night My cross. Do not be afraid of My cross. Embrace the cross and you will embrace My Father's will for you. Through that cross comes joy, and peace, and salvation. I give you My mercy to wipe out the fear in your heart. I am with you. I AM ALWAYS WITH YOU!

Notes & Reflections:

JANUARY 23, 1992
MESSAGE FROM OUR LADY

My dear children, I come to ask you to pray and to love. I come because my Son is love, and He loves you all, His beloved children. My dear little ones, begin first to love your family. Be love to one another, then you can love your fellow brethren. Please beware that Satan is trying to cause division and disrupt unity not only in the family, but in the world. Form together in love as a strong unit and you will have the shield to protect you against his attempts. I love you, my little ones, and bless you in the name of my Son. Thank you for responding to my call.

Notes & Reflections:

JANUARY 30, 1992
MESSAGE FROM OUR LADY

My dear little ones, I, your Mother of Joy, come to comfort you and bless you in the name of my Son. My dear children, be calm little children, loving and at peace. The control you wish to have can only be the control my Son gives you in His peace and love. Surrender to Him and trust Him. He will guide you and crown you with His love. Dear, dear children, pray for surrendering and to be the open vessels of my Son's love. I bless you, my dear ones. Thank you for your response to my call.
Notes & Reflections:

JANUARY 30, 1992
MESSAGE FROM OUR LORD

My dear ones, I ask you this night for your faithfulness and your perseverance. Please allow Me, your Jesus, to be your God. Trust Me please. I ask for your faithfulness and your perseverance because with those I will be able to touch you. Without faithfulness you block My touch. I am here with you. I am with you wherever you are. Please allow Me to be your God. As you allow this through your faithfulness and perseverance, then you will be able to receive the gifts that I offer to you and I long to give you - peace, compassion and My mercy! I thank you for your devotion. I know, my dear ones, it is not easy. That is why I am with you, and that is why My mother is here. You are never alone. You are mine and I love you!
Notes & Reflections:

FEBRUARY 6, 1992
MESSAGE FROM OUR LADY

My dear children, do not be preoccupied with worry. Trust in my Son. Surrender unto Him all your worries, concerns and fears and be at peace. You are weak in your humanness, but strong in my Son. Seek to serve Him faithfully, being obedient and loving in following His ways. He has taught you. I love you, my dear little children. I am your Mother of Joy to bring you the joy of my Son. I bless you and thank you for responding to my call.
Notes & Reflections:

FEBRUARY 6, 1992
MESSAGE FROM OUR LORD

My dear ones, I come to you this night to speak to you once again of the simplicity of following My call. My dear ones, I invite you to trust, trust in Me and in My Father and in Our Holy Spirit. When you trust, then fear disappears. I want for you the peace that I am so willing to give you. You will experience this peace in simplicity. My words to you have never been complicated. They have been plain and simple; and when you listen to them with your heart, you know the truth. I love you and I encourage you this night to simplicity in following My call. I AM ALWAYS, ALWAYS WITH YOU!

Notes & Reflections:

FEBRUARY 13, 1992
MESSAGE FROM OUR LADY

My dear children, please pray for my priests. Pray, pray, pray. Never cease praying. Do not cause division but unite in harmony and be obedient to my beloved Pope. Please, my little children, pray that division does not result from lack of love, and power of human ways. This will only deepen the sorrow of my heart. I love you, my dear ones, and I bless you in the name of my Son. Thank you for responding to my call.

Notes & Reflections:

FEBRUARY 20, 1992
MESSAGE FROM OUR LADY

My dear children, I am here because my Son is here. I am not leaving because my Son is here and He is not leaving. His divine mercy and love is flowing out unto you and all your beloved ones. Oh, my dear little ones, NO obstacle is too great for my Son. Give to Him your fears, anxieties and worries. Open and surrender to Him. Please, my dear ones, as you receive my Son this night, be intimate with Him so that He can fill you with discernment and His peace. I bless you, my dear little children. Thank you for responding to my call.

Notes & Reflections:

FEBRUARY 20, 1992
MESSAGE FROM OUR LORD

My dear ones, I come to you again this night to speak to your heart. I remind you that I, your Lord and Saviour, do not look at your outward trappings, I look at your heart. Please believe Me when I say to you - I love you as you are. So often I see that you do not love yourself. My dear ones, I accept you as you are at this moment. I love you, YOU, not your actions. I see that you look so often at your actions and you are overcome by your weaknesses and by your sinfulness.

My dear ones, only when you love and accept yourself as you are and offer yourself to me AS YOU ARE, only then will My love for you be able to flow into your very heart. Again, I say to you, believe that I love you, believe that I love you so much that even now I will do anything not to have you separated from Me. Accept My love and offer Me this night yourself. I take you all in My embrace. YOU ARE MINE!

Notes & Reflections:

FEBRUARY 27, 1992
MESSAGE FROM OUR LADY

My dear children, I come to be here with you because I come with my Son. I bless you this night. Please, my dear ones, FOCUS completely on my Son. If you are totally immersed in His love, focusing on Him, all your disturbances would dissipate because you would be in His peace. You cannot control, my dear ones, because my Son is here. Even if you think you are right, and are not correct, the truth of my Son's light would be made known. Therefore, focus totally on Him and do not allow trivial disturbances to disrupt your peace. Focus and pray, pray, pray. Thank you for responding to my call.
Notes & Reflections:

FEBRUARY 27, 1992
MESSAGE FROM OUR LORD

My dear ones, I come tonight to you to invite you to give Me, your Lord, the totality of your heart. Allow Me to be your wealth. I see how hard you try and how so often distraction clouds your vision of Me. My dear ones, I am with you now and forever. I am as close to you as your heart because you have invited Me to be your heart. I love you and because of my love for you, I give you My Kingdom. Pray, persevere! I am with you. I give you this night the love, and the healing, and the strength. I gift you Myself and I take your heart and present it to My Father. Be at peace. I calm your worried heart.
Notes & Reflections:

MARCH 5, 1992
MESSAGE FROM OUR LADY

My dear children, I came to ask you for reconciliation. I, your mother, see so many broken hearts. Please be open to begin more time for confessions here at this parish for all my children coming. My priests, I call from afar, please be open to assisting My chosen pastor in making this available for my children to receive this most beautiful sacrament. It is necessary here at my Son's Center of His Divine Mercy so that He can free you and heal you. Please by obedient to this, my Son's request. I love you, my dear little children, and bless you in the name of He Who sent me. Pray and prepare for your new beginning through confession. Thank you for responding to this my Son's call.
Notes & Reflections:

MARCH 5, 1992
MESSAGE FROM OUR LORD

My dear little ones, I come to you this night to ask you to choose life. My dear ones, I do not wish that you die. I came and I am now here to offer you life in the fullest measure. Choose life by choosing to follow Me, your Jesus. You follow Me, my dear ones, by giving up your sinfulness. You see, your sinfulness blocks you from My loving embrace because you have chosen to embrace a thing or a person instead of Me. My dear ones, embrace Me. Live! I gift you this night the grace and the strength you need to turn from sin. Come, embrace Me, so that I may embrace you and you will live forever with Me. Don't give up. Take My hand. I am with you. During these days I give you My mother in a very special way. Use her as your example of choosing life. I love her! I love her! SHE BRINGS YOU TO ME! I LOVE HER!

Notes & Reflections:

MARCH 12, 1992
MESSAGE FROM OUR LADY

My dear children, seek a private and personal intimacy with my Son. He desires your love and for an intimate quiet relationship with each one of you. My dear little children, do not delay in running to my Son. Use the most blessed sacrament of confession and trust that your journey is in the best hands.

My dear children, during this season, do not be somber or afraid but rejoice that my Son is your Saviour and believe it. Trust in Him. Use the sacrament please, my dear ones, of reconciliation; and trust, pray, pray, love and surrender in peace unto my Son. Thank you, my children, for responding to my call.

Notes & Reflections:

MARCH 12, 1992
MESSAGE FROM OUR LORD

My dear ones, I am here with you, your Jesus of Mercy. You are not alone, never alone. I am with you! Our Holy Spirit is within you always! I send My angels to guard you and, in this time, I have even sent My mother to be with you. My Father gives you these gifts because He loves you. He invites you again, over and over again to believe in His love. I give you this night the grace of My mercy and I touch your heart. I invite you to come into My heart and to be at peace with Me. Now you can go because you are strengthened. You have nothing to fear. I AM WITH YOU!

Notes & Reflections:

MARCH 19, 1992
MESSAGE FROM OUR LADY

My dear children, as I read your hearts this night, I bless you and invite you to allow me to comfort your sadness. My dear little ones, your trials and tribulations shall pass. Receive them in joy, not in sadness. See my Son as your strength. Please, little ones, it is time to pray, not to cry. Trust, again I say, trust in my Son. Do not be afraid. I am here and my Son

is here, so be at peace as my Son molds you into His beautiful creation. Blessings on you and thank you for responding to my call.
Notes & Reflections:

MARCH 19, 1992
MESSAGE FROM OUR LORD

My dear ones, I am here with you this night to invite you to be My disciples of hope. I see in the hearts of My people a lack of that gift that I wish to give them, as I give it to you. And so, I invite you to live in the spirit of hope for the world, to be signs for them of My salvation, to be signs for them, that through their suffering, there is joy. My dear ones, you will only be disciples of hope as you become obedient to My Father, as I was obedient not only to My Father but to my dear, dear Joseph. Without obedience there is no hope. I love you and thank you for listening to Me. Your effect on those to whom I send you is already having a wonderful end. I bless you this night, My dear ones, and I strengthen your hope as I strengthen your obedience. Together we are obedient always to God, Our Father.
Notes & Reflections:

MARCH 26, 1992
MESSAGE FROM OUR LADY

My dear children, reach out to one another. Be kind, and loving, and compassionate. You are sharp with one another, judging, and you need to love. Focus on my Son, and you will be molded in His love so that you will be able to love each other. Do not focus on your skepticism or worry about who is right or who is wrong. But if you focus on your own journey with my Jesus, you will have peace and He will guide you. God's will will be done and His truth will be revealed. Please love, my little ones. I bless you and take your petitions to my Son. Thank you for responding to my call.
Notes & Reflections:

MARCH 26, 1992
MESSAGE FROM OUR LORD

My dear ones, My Father again sends Me this night to you, as He has sent Me before to invite and to teach you, to draw you closer, to draw your world back to Him. I thank you this night for listening to My voice. You do not see Me, but you can hear Me. Thank you for listening. Thank you for accepting My presence here with you. Because of your acceptance, you are able to hear when I speak. I invite you this night to give to Me your pride-filled hearts which are full of hurt. Give them to Me, and I will heal them and give you new hearts. Because of your acceptance of My presence with you, My Father continues to allow Me to speak. He allows My mother to be with you. Because of this blessing that you have given to My Father, He blesses you this night through Me. He gives you the strength, and His grace, and His

mercy. Because of your acceptance, these tremendous gifts go out from you to all. I love you. Thank you for allowing Me to touch your heart.
Notes & Reflections:

APRIL 2, 1992
MESSAGE FROM OUR LADY

My dear children, I am your mother, your medium to my Son, Jesus, the Alpha and the Omega. My dear little ones, please pay attention to your own journey instead of helping others with their spiritual journey. My Jesus wishes to guide each of you personally on your own journey, if you will allow Him. I protect you and prepare you in perfection for my Son. He will not deny you His love because He will not deny me, and I present you to Him like a little child. Please do not judge others of pridefulness when this is only harboring bitterness in your own hearts. They are truly humble, but it is your own pride surfacing. Therefore, please pay attention to your own walk with my Son, and He will purify you and grace you with His virtues. Thank you, my little ones, for responding to my call.
Notes & Reflections:

APRIL 2, 1992
MESSAGE FROM OUR LORD

My dear ones, I, your Jesus, am here with you this night because of the love of My Father whom I have told you is your Father also. He sends Me to you to plead on His behalf to invite you again to come to Him. You listen. My Father thanks you for listening. My dear ones, I ask that you pray for those who do not listen, who have filled themselves so full of themselves that they have no room for My Father's words. Listen as I speak to you within your heart. My dear ones, there is nothing to fear. Live what you have heard from Me who speaks only what My Father wishes. I am here this night to remind you not only of My love, but of God the Father's love for you. I bless you with My mercy which is His mercy, with My peace which is His peace. WE LOVE YOU! WE LOVE YOU! WE LOVE YOU!
Notes & Reflections:

APRIL 9, 1992
MESSAGE FROM OUR LADY

My dear children, I am your Mother of Joy because my Son is my joy. He is your joy. Give to Him your hearts, dear ones. Please allow Him to comfort you, hold you and guide you in the only true journey to true happiness and eternal bliss. My dear little ones, God does exist. Unite now together in love. Do not wait for signs and wonders. If you wait, it will be too late. Turn now to my Son. During this week, go to my Son and immerse yourself into His Most Sacred Heart. The urgency is prayer and conversion to the truth NOW! Do not fear.

There is no need to fear, but need to change. Thank you, my dear children, for responding to my call.

Notes & Reflections:

APRIL 9, 1992
MESSAGE FROM OUR LORD

My dear ones, I invite you to walk with Me this week the steps I took to gain your freedom. Embrace with Me the cross, the sign of your freedom, and the covenant with God, My Father and yours, made again with you. As you embrace the cross, you will also embrace the resurrection. I love you! This week you will see again the depth of My love. You will experience again, when you open your hearts, the depth of My mercy. You need not fear the cross. I am with you always - always with you. My dear little ones, come to Me and together we will go to My Father and to your Father. I love you. KNOW THAT I LOVE YOU!

Notes & Reflections:

APRIL 23, 1992
MESSAGE FROM OUR LADY

My dear little children, I come to give you the blessing of my Son. Please, focus on Him. Unite together and pray for peace. Please be loving. Satan is trying to cause division. Please be alert, my children. Pray, pray, pray. Join Me. Join together in love. Stop your bickering and judging of others. Pray, be silent and loving. Join with me. Reconcile, my children. I have asked three times now, from my Son, for the sacrament of reconciliation to take place here at His Center of Mercy. Please take action, reconcile and join to a peaceful end. I love you and bless you, my little children. Thank you for your response to my call.

Notes & Reflections:

APRIL 23, 1992
MESSAGE FROM OUR LORD

My dear ones, I am with you here and now! I, your Resurrected Lord, your Jesus of Mercy, am here. You say that you cannot see Me. I say to you do not look for Me with your eyes but with your heart. Go into the silence of your heart where I am waiting for you. There you will see Me. There will I embrace you; and, in the silence, we are one. I invite you to come away with Me into your heart so that I may heal you, embrace you with My peace, and joy, and mercy. I AM HERE! I have always been with you since My Father raised Me from death to life. Allow Me to enliven you. Look and see with your heart. This night I touch your heart. I hold it so that you may come to Me, so that you may receive the embrace that I long to give to you. Be silent and see me!

Notes & Reflections:

APRIL 30, 1992
MESSAGE FROM OUR LADY

My dear children, pray for your enemies and bless those who persecute you. Allow the Spirit of God to move through you out unto others. Any blessing you extend out to others will be returned to you if not received well from the other person. So send a loving prayer to your enemies, and that love and peace will only come to rest on you if not received in openness from those you pray for. Have mercy, my dear ones, have mercy. Mercy is the unquestionable proof of your love for God. Unite in love. I bless you in the name of my Son. Thank you for responding to my call.
Notes & Reflections:

APRIL 30, 1992
MESSAGE FROM OUR LORD

I come again this night to you, sent again by My heavenly Father. I am with you. I say again this night to your heart -- do not be afraid. Take My hand. I will never abandon you. I am with you now and will be with you always. Do not fear. Be with Me totally. I love you and I bless you with My presence which is My Spirit within you. You are strong because of the Holy Spirit. Peace! My mercy is upon you this night.
Notes & Reflections:

MAY 7, 1992
MESSAGE FROM OUR LADY

My dear little children, those who are begotten of God conquer the world. You conquer through faith, love and trust in Him. My dear little ones, I come because my Son's love is upon you. Please unite and live in harmony. Be loving and kind. Be compassionate. Focus on Him. Thank the Father for it is His love that you are so beautiful. Pray, my dear ones, pray for peace and forgive one another. I bless you tonight in the name of my Son. Thank you for responding to my Son. Come now into His most Sacred Heart. He awaits your love. Peace!
Notes & Reflections:

MAY 7, 1992
MESSAGE FROM OUR LORD

My dear ones, I come to you this night to tell you that I am your life. I, your Jesus, am your food. I come to tell you of My love with all of My heart. I love you, each of you. I ask you -- accept Me as your life, as your food. You are precious to Me. I bless you this night, the blessing that goes into your very soul -- blessing and healing and mercy, compassion and joy,

and truth and courage, and above all, hope and faith. I am with you. There is nothing at all to fear. Take My hand, I want to hold you.
Notes & Reflections:

MAY 14, 1992
MESSAGE FROM OUR LORD

My dear ones, I am here with you again this night to remind you of My love, to invite you to accept that love again fully into your hearts. The love with which I love you is a selfless, self-sacrificing love. My Father gives Me again this night to you. I come to invite you to be My apostle of love, each of you -- each of you to love those to whom I send you to be My apostle of hope to those dear ones.

Yes, my dear little ones, it will not be easy to love and to be hopeful unless you allow My love and My hope to be yours. I need you to touch your world. You are now My apostles, the ones I send. If you accept -- if you accept, know that I am with you. I am always with you. Please believe Me when I say again, "I have chosen you." Pray to accept this invitation.
Notes & Reflections:

MAY 21, 1992
MESSAGE FROM OUR LADY

My dear little children, it brings me joy to see you praying. Pray! Pray! Pray! I take your prayers to Jesus Who presents you to the Father. My dear ones, prayer is the powerful tool to prevent dissension and confusion from the evil one. My children, please unite. Do not look at the past, but unite now in the moment and on-going from this point together. Do not try to control or be stubborn. These only bring self-destruction, not spiritual freedom. I love you, little ones, and bless you in the name of my Son. Thank you for responding to my call.
Notes & Reflections:

MAY 21, 1992
MESSAGE FROM OUR LORD

My dear ones, I come to you this night to remind you that I have given you My joy. I wish you to have this gift of joy to the fullest measure. The reason you do not experience this joy is because so often you do not keep My commandments. When you do not keep My commandments, you block the joy that I give you. Instead of joy, you experience pain and confusion and chaos in your life. I, your Jesus of Mercy, beg you this night to keep My commandments so that you may experience My joy. My Father and I send My mother to you under the title of Joy to remind you that this is the gift that you can have. My dear ones, I love you. When I see you not keeping My commandments, when I see the pain and the confusion and the chaos that this causes in your life, it saddens Me. I tell you it doesn't have to be that way. This night I have reminded you of the way to possess this joy. Please listen

and act on it. I strengthen you with My mercy to overcome your sinfulness; and I give you the gift of My peace.
Notes & Reflections:

MAY 28, 1992
MESSAGE FROM OUR LADY

My dear little children, in Jesus I love you and come in the blessings of my Son. Please, my little ones, pray fervently and be at peace living in the moment. Be loving and patient. Tonight I pass on the special blessing of my Son to you. Pass on to one another this blessing through love. Embrace my Son by embracing one another in love. Unite and live in harmony. Pray, my little ones, pray! The evil one is trying to cause destruction. Only prayer and love are the swords to freedom and justice in God. I bless you in the name of my Son. Treasure Him. Love Him by loving one another. Thank you for responding to my call.
Notes & Reflections:

JUNE 4, 1992
MESSAGE FROM OUR LADY

My dear children, Jesus loves you. He is my dear Son, my dear Jesus. In the midst of your world there are struggles and hardships, but all can be overcome because Jesus has overcome the world. My son exists amongst you and He is calling you to remove yourself from focusing on your hardship and the business of your life, but to focus on Him and trust in Him. All love is of Him and all must be yielded to Him in love to live in union with Him in His peace.

I bless you, my little, little ones, and encourage you this night to give all of yourself to Jesus in commitment of love. There is nothing you risk when you give to Him your total being as He has given to you. Pray and love, my little ones. Give to Him in love of yourself. He is real. Thank you for your response. Peace can exist if you begin to live peacefully and unselfishly. Blessings in the name of He Who has sent me.
Notes & Reflections:

JUNE 4, 1992
MESSAGE FROM OUR LORD

My dear ones, I come to you this night to encourage you to speak the truth and to live the truth. This truth is the gift that I give to you with My Father and through Our Holy Spirit. You will know the truth as you listen with your heart to the ways in which My Father and Myself and Our Holy Spirit speak to you. You live My truth when you keep My commandments. My dear ones, live simply, speak less and let your words always give honor and glory to My Father. I look upon you this night with the most tender love of My heart, and I see that you are yearning to be truly children of My Father. I tell you, My dear ones, one of the signs that you are truly children of God is that you live and speak the truth. In this world of the evil one's deceptions, you will stand out as a light as you live and speak the truth. I give you My strength to live this gift of truth. I touch your minds, and your lips, and your hearts, so that you may speak the truth of Our God, of My Father and your Father. And as you speak and live the truth, know that My Father and Our Holy Spirit and I are with you and within you, as close to you as your very breath.

Notes & Reflections:

JUNE 11, 1992
MESSAGE FROM OUR LADY

My dear little children, peace to you and blessings in the name of my Son. My dear ones, I need to continue to invite you to daily prayer and focus on my Son. Trust in Him, my little ones. All will be well and you will live in His most Sacred Heart if you love Him and allow Him to love you. Trust, my dear ones, and pray. Never cease praying. There is much destruction in the world, but Jesus is peace and love, if all unite and put aside trivial arguments. I love you and bless you in the name of Jesus. Peace. Thank you for responding to my call.

Notes & Reflections:

JUNE 11, 1992
MESSAGE FROM OUR LORD

My dear ones, I am here again with you this night to remind you that I am always in your heart. I invite you ever more to come to Me within your own heart to allow My presence to become more and more real to you. My dear ones, I am the gift that My Father gives to you. I invite you again to accept Me, your Saviour and the Lord of your heart. Experience, My dear ones, My presence within you as you pray, and together we will praise My Father and your Father. Pray, My dear ones, with your heart, and you will find that I am with you. I bless you with My presence, with My peace and with My mercy.

Notes & Reflections:

JUNE 18, 1992
MESSAGE FROM OUR LADY

My dear ones, I love you. My Jesus taught you how to pray. He has allowed me to come to you to invite you to pray with your heart. My dear little ones, so often you say that you do not know how to pray. Listen to my Jesus speak to your hearts. Listen as my spouse, the Holy Spirit speaks to your heart. They will again teach you. Come and pray. I invite you even more this night to pray. Please believe me when I say to you how valuable prayer from your heart is. Your prayer is capable of changing not only events but the hardest of hearts as well. I am with you here, and wherever you go I will pray with you. I invite you to pray with

me. I love you, my dear little ones, with the love of a mother's heart. I embrace you and draw each of you close to my heart, my heart which is my Son, Jesus. May His name be praised now and forever more.
Notes & Reflections:

JULY 2, 1992
MESSAGE FROM OUR LORD

My dear ones, as you come here this night to pray, so many ask for healing. I tell you, My dear ones, I wish to heal all of you, but what each of you needs healing of most, you very seldom ask for healing. That area, My dear ones, is the area of your sin. Your sin destroys you; your sin paralyzes you; your sin is the cancer of your soul. My dear ones, I ask you and invite you now to give to Me your sin so that I may heal you truly. I love you. I have died for you, My Father has raised Me up for you. It is truly simple, My dear ones, stop sinning and you will be healed - healed in your spirit, healed within your heart. Do not be discouraged, My dear ones, by your sin. Offer your sin to Me. I will heal you. I love you and bless you this night with My peace, with My forgiveness, and with My mercy.
Notes & Reflections:

JULY 23, 1992
MESSAGE FROM OUR LORD

My dear ones, I come this night to remind you again that I am here. I am with you. At times, because you have chosen to be your own god, you do not experience Me. My little ones, open your hearts. Open your hearts so that you may understand that I, your Jesus, wish to be the Lord in your heart so that I may lead you back to God. My dear ones, when you are so preoccupied with yourselves, with your selfishness, with your pride, and with your pain, I cannot be the Lord in your heart. I love you and I extend again My arms to you. I am here with you. I am with you in your heart. Allow Me to be your Lord once more. Give me this night the pride, the selfishness, the pain, so that I may once again reign in your heart, and then we, together, will go to My Father. Peace and joy, My dear ones.
Notes & Reflections:

JULY 30, 1992
MESSAGE FROM OUR LORD

My dear ones, I come this night to tell you that you are not useless to My Father nor to Me. You are precious to Me, each of you, and to My Father, to your Father. You are beautiful to us. We love you. I ask you this night to allow Our Holy Spirit to mold your heart - to mold it, to form it, and to offer it to God Our Father. To each of you who are here I bless you with My grace and the grace of God Our Father. Know that in the remolding of your heart, although it will be painful at times, I am there. I love you and bless you and take you, each of you, to My heart.

Notes & Reflections:

AUGUST 6, 1992
MESSAGE FROM OUR LADY

My dear children, pray! Pray! Pray! Oh my dear ones, I need your prayers in this critical time of my plan. Please continue to open your hearts to my Son. Continue to surrender your own wills to the Divine will of the Father. My little, little children, I love you so! You fill me with so much joy as you pray for all the lost souls of your world. I love you. Peace to you. Thank you for responding to my call.

Notes & Reflections:

AUGUST 13, 1992
MESSAGE FROM OUR LADY

My dear little, little children, be not afraid! Know that my Son and I are guiding you. Please continue to take hold of our hands and allow us to lead you down the path of salvation. What is needed now is trust and much prayer! I love you, my little ones, and know I am your mother! Thank you for responding to my call.

Notes & Reflections:

AUGUST 27, 1992
MESSAGE FROM OUR LADY
TO THE WORLD

My dear children, I urge your close attention as my Son has allowed me to be here. Please, my little ones, put aside your falsehoods and fears. There is too much negativity acting as a catalyst to human destruction. I invite you instead to draw closer to one another in prayer -- renew prayer in the family and devotion to spending more time with Jesus. IT IS URGENT! There are great struggles about to unfold. Division in families is leading to divisions in the Church. Reconciliation is URGENT! I have asked prayer, conversion, penance, and initially you took steps to procure your relationship with God, but are reverting to old ways. I have asked for obedience to my Pope, but division is resulting.

The need for prayer, reconciliation, harmony, love and conversion is URGENT NOW! Renounce what is preventing you in your spiritual growth. Read the holy scripture and listen to the Holy Spirit speak the message of my Son. Begin right now to solidify your relationship with God by loving yourselves and restoring your self respect. Cease from running from yourselves. You cannot love your countrymen if you do not love yourself. You are walking ways of power instead of love. The greatest sin is that which destroys love. THIS IS URGENT! The effects of this wickedness is causing jealousy, hatred, killings and divisions.

The war, power struggles and economical warfares are surfacing from lack of love. My Son is tired, very tired. The faith of God is forgotten.

The time is coming when every man and woman on this earth will know that God exists. All will have a glimpse at the state of their soul. Those seconds will seem like eternity. Your love of gold and silver is about to become glittering dust and be swept away.

Spiritual warfare exists in the Heavens, and you must now live in the perfection of your faith. The wicked are convinced they are invisible, but they are not. Do not be afraid. To all his faithful ones, God promises victory over the powers of evil and the world. Know, my little ones, that only God can make you holy. You can receive God's seal on your soul only by abandoning your will to Him. God's love will shower you and replace everything if you accept it.

Bless you, my little ones, and thank you for responding to my URGENT call.
Notes & Reflections:

AUGUST 27, 1992
MESSAGE FROM OUR LORD

My dear beloved ones, I come this night from My Father to encourage you and to invite you again to continue your journey. There is nothing that you need to fear. I am with you always! I am with you when you are alone; I am with you when you are with your families; I am with you at work; I am with you at school; I am with you all the time, everywhere. My dear ones, what is there for you to fear? Nothing -- there is nothing for you to fear. Do you fear death? By dying I have conquered death for you. Are you in fear because of your sin? My dear ones, by dying I destroyed sin and the hold that sin would have upon you. I have conquered everything and yet I know, My dear ones, how difficult it is for you because you do not see Me.

I am here to tell you that you are looking for Me in the wrong place. Come to Me in My Blessed Sacrament; I am there! Listen to Me through the sacred scriptures; I am there! And if you allow yourself the quiet that I would give you, you will find Me within your heart. There is nothing to fear.

This night I bless you and ask you to give to me again your heart for I give you mine! Peace, mercy, My strength, the joy of our Holy Spirit is with you always.
Notes & Reflections:

SEPTEMBER 3, 1992
MESSAGE FROM OUR LADY

My dear children, I am your mother who comes tonight to wrap you in my mantle of love. Oh, my children, PLEASE do not fear. Fear is useless, my little ones. Pray for peace, peace in your own hearts. By praying for peace, you can conquer any fear or temptation. I love

you, my little ones! Please pray for peace for yourselves, and you will bring that peace to the whole world.
Notes & Reflections:

SEPTEMBER 3, 1992
MESSAGE FROM OUR LORD

My dear ones, I come to you this night -- I, your merciful Lord, to ask and to invite you again to put Me first in your life, so that I may lead you to My Father Who is your Father. My dear little ones, I see in your heart so much worry for others, so much sadness for others. I tell you if only you will pray and allow Me to be the center of your heart, and no one else, I would then be able to take care of those for whom you worry and those who are causing you sadness. My dear ones, please take care of yourself and your relationship with Me. Allow that to be the most important thing in your life, and you will then be truly children of My Father.

This night I offer you, if you would only take, My strength, to give up the worry for others. My dear, dear ones, don't you understand that if you are worried you will be distracted? I love those for whom you worry and those who cause you sadness more than you could possibly imagine. Give them to Me. This night especially give Me again your heart. I give you My mercy, I give you My peace, and I give you again this night My heart -- My mother! I love you! I love you! My dear ones, truly MY LOVE IS ALL YOU NEED!
Notes & Reflections:

SEPTEMBER 10, 1992
MESSAGE FROM OUR LADY

My dear children, I am your Mother of Joy, but also your Mother of Sorrows. I see your pain and your sufferings, my little ones. I ask you to unite your tears with the most precious blood of my Son's passion. I ask you to allow Him to soften your hearts and to allow your purification to continue. I love you, my dear children. Please continue to pray for the lost souls of the world. Peace to you.
Notes & Reflections:

SEPTEMBER 10, 1992
MESSAGE FROM OUR LORD

My dear ones, I come to you this night to say one thing to you -- I wish to encourage you in your following Me. My commandment of love is not easy for you. As you draw closer to Me, I will be able to love more through you, but it is not easy, my dear ones. It truly is a labor -- a labor of love. There are people in your life who are easy to love -- cherish them, but there are also people in your life who are not easy to love. Those are the ones, My dear

ones, to whom I send you. I will love them through you. I will be with you. I will strengthen you. You will not be alone. I was rejected when I tried to love. My dear ones, so too will you be rejected. Cling to Me and even the rejection will not be as painful. Know that to love is My commandment still for you. This night I touch that part of your heart which has been hurt as you attempted to love and have been rejected. I heal you and bless you and take you to My heart. My dear ones, I, your Lord, love you, and I will never reject you.
Notes & Reflections:

SEPTEMBER 17, 1992
MESSAGE FROM OUR LADY

My dear children, I continue to call you to unity and harmony. The evil one is trying desperately to cause division, and work in every circumstance towards deception and darkness. If you would listen and act on what I ask, you will be protected from all harm. Begin practicing and living my words to you in your own life. Do not be fearful and do not dwell on negativity. Instead, abandon fully to my Son. Nothing is safer than the way of self abandonment. True faith allows you to accept with joy everything that happens. If you abandon unto my Son, the results will be glorious. God will grace you in every moment to act virtuously. God's action is boundless in scope and power. Empty yourselves so my Son can fill you. Thank you, my little ones, my blessings in the name of my Son and His peace. To His name be praise and glory. Thank you for responding to my call.
Notes & Reflections:

SEPTEMBER 17, 1992
MESSAGE FROM OUR LORD

My dear ones, I come this night as your Lord and Saviour, the Jesus of Mercy whom you follow, to ask again, to invite once again that you love Me. My dear ones, the way you love Me is to pray. This simple request -- in fulfilling it you show your love for Me. I see so many of you, you are so busy about so many things, even busy about holy things, but in your busyness you are putting prayer aside. My dear ones, pray first, and always, and during, and last. I know you do not understand the power of prayer, of your prayer. My mother has told you, and is telling you, and begged you to pray. I, your Lord, ask you now -- pray, rededicate your lives to prayer. It is truly, My dear ones, believe Me, the most important thing that you can do for anyone; that you can do for the world. It is the holiest of holy works.

I ask you this night to put prayer back into the place where it belongs in your life. I know too, my dear ones, how taxing it may be, but if you do it for Me you will experience My peace and My joy, and you will then be able to see clearly what truly I am asking of you in your lives. I bless you with My love, I bless you and your family with My mercy.
Notes & Reflections:

SEPTEMBER 24, 1992
MESSAGE FROM OUR LADY

My dear little children, a holy soul is one which freely submits to God's will. By the help of His grace self-abandonment will follow. Live in peace and do not be frightened. Know for certain that God is guiding you. You may not understand or see clearly God's works but, if you abandon unto Him, you will see clearly the action of His grace. God loves you, my little ones. He is love and love inspires you to perform your duties faithfully and with love. Pray for His strength of joy and offer your distress with joy to God. You may not understand His methods or solve His puzzles, but you will attain full beauty and rejoice as He conquers your despair. Bless you, my little ones, and thank you for responding to my call.
Notes & Reflections:

OCTOBER 1, 1992
MESSAGE FROM OUR LADY

My dear children, do not be upset or worried from the humiliation which comes from this present world. Shelter in our God and enjoy Him who lives in you. You can benefit from your weaknesses and failures, fears and doubts, by drawing good from your infirmities. My Son wishes to be your only nourishment and desire. God is your only sole support and only means of achieving holiness. Thank you, my dear little ones, for responding to my call. Peace to you. Blessings from my Son are upon you.
Notes & Reflections:

OCTOBER 1, 1992
MESSAGE FROM OUR LORD

My dear ones, I invite you this night to come to Me as children of My Father. I ask you again this night to trust in His will for you as I trusted, as My mother trusted. This trust will assist you in living as the children of God. I am here with you to remind you of the love My Father has for you. He sent Me once and now he sends Me again. I am with you. I tell you I love you also. Dear children of My Father, I bless you with My peace and with My mercy.
Notes & Reflections:

OCTOBER 8, 1992
MESSAGE FROM OUR LADY

My dear little children, I your Mother of Joy have come for a purpose. My little ones I am the mother of this country. This is my country and I need your help. As you seek me, I also seek your help. Please, my little ones, there needs to be great conversion and change of heart, unity and harmony. I need you. You are the ones that can change this country's situation and be the catalyst for change in the world. Pray, pray, pray. Take heed to change your hearts and return back to God. Be living examples of God's word. Live the gospel. Live my

Son's words. I bless you, my little ones, and ask for your help. Thank you for responding to my call.

Notes & Reflections:

OCTOBER 8, 1992
MESSAGE FROM OUR LORD

My dear ones, I am here with you. I, your Jesus of Mercy, to tell you again this night of My love for you and to remind you that you are not alone. I bless you this night with My mercy. My dear ones, I see your hearts. I see your hearts not as you see them but as My Father sees them, and I take your hearts to My heart to heal them, to strengthen them, to give them again joy and hope. I ask you to persevere in your love, to persevere in the hope that I give you, to persevere in your prayer. I am with you. You are children of My Father. We love you. We love you.

Notes & Reflections:

OCTOBER 15, 1992
MESSAGE FROM OUR LADY

My dear children, I am your mother! Please PRAY, PRAY, PRAY! Pray for Jesus to put the desire to sacrifice in your heart -- to sacrifice for your sins and the lost souls of the world. Please, my children, be humble and obedient! Please pray and sacrifice for the love of my Jesus. I love you. Peace to you. Thank you for listening to my words.

Notes & Reflections:

OCTOBER 22, 1992
MESSAGE FROM OUR LADY

My dear children, do not set limits on the will of God. The will of God is the life of the body and the soul. His will is good and true, and those who possess Him need nothing else. God's will is all powerful and wise. Those who trust completely without reservations have firm confidence and faith in Him. Do not seek other things or try to link events with God's designs, but surrender to Him blindly and with confidence. All that is graced upon you will produce individual fruits. My little ones, my blessing is upon you in the name of my Jesus. Thank you for responding to my call.

Notes & Reflections:

OCTOBER 22, 1992
MESSAGE FROM OUR LORD

My dear ones, I am with you this night so put all fear aside. I am with you, there is no need to be anxious. The division that My presence brought and still brings to you is the division of choice between God and the world. I present you to My Father. The reason that He sent Me was to tell you that He is your Father also, and this is where the division comes.

My dear ones, there is only one God, My Father and I, His only Son, and Our Holy Spirit. As I present you to God Our Father, your hearts are blessed and strengthened. Thank you, my dear ones, for choosing God. Know that in this choice others will be divided from you, that I am with you. I always take you to My Father. You are not alone. I bless you this night with My mercy and My peace.
Notes & Reflections:

OCTOBER 29, 1992
MESSAGE FROM OUR LADY

My dear little children, constantly pursue my Son and you will find Him. Be faithful, happy and seeking souls advancing after my beloved Son. Remain faithful at the foot of the cross. Increase your love and adoration of him. Venerate Him in untiring pursuit through all the disguises. Pass through the shadows and veils which may try to hide the will of my Son. Follow Jesus. Love Him and pray with all your heart. Pray! Please pray. Much has been mitigated because of prayer and conversion. Continue, my little ones. Everything is contingent upon prayer. Thank you for responding to my call.
Notes & Reflections:

OCTOBER 29, 1992
MESSAGE FROM OUR LORD

My dear ones, I am here again this night with you to say very plainly and to speak to your heart -- know for certain that there is a war going on at this moment for your soul. The warfare is intense and yet, My dear ones, it is so subtle that many are being lulled into a state of complacency. In this warfare I say to you there is nothing for you to fear. I am with you, but I beg you this night to stay with Me. Be with Me, for with Me there is peace for you, and there is strength and there is hope. The devil is trying in every way to lure you from Me to destroy you. If you stay with Me, you will never be destroyed. As you stay with Me, you will be purified. I love you with My heart and I bless you this night again with My mercy. Stay with Me, and you will be saved.
Notes & Reflections:

NOVEMBER 5, 1992
MESSAGE FROM OUR LADY

My dear little children, praised be Jesus. My little ones, Jesus not only gives freedom but also new life, a life you cannot attain by your own efforts. Do not trust in your own weak desire to take you to God, but place all your trust and confidence in His desire for you. You must remove yourself from the tensions of control and surrender completely. Ground yourself firmly on His absolute goodness and fidelity and not on your own feelings.

I love you, my dear little ones. My Son loves you. He has allowed me to be here with you. It is my prayer for you that Jesus will bring you to perfect fulfillment in Him. Thank you for your response to my call.

Notes & Reflections:

NOVEMBER 5, 1992
MESSAGE FROM OUR LORD

My dear ones, I have come this night to where you are to tell you once again you are mine! My Father has given you to Me. My dear ones, in so many ways I see how lost you still are, so distracted, so put upon, still so worried. When you allow those things to overcome you, you are lost and you are isolating yourself. I am here with you now this night to tell you take courage when you are beset with worry, when you are distracted, when you are fearful. Come to Me in My most Blessed Sacrament; and there you will not only find Me, but you will find your true self. I will be with you always. I am with you now.

I ask you to thank My Father, and yours, that He has allowed Me to be with you for such a time, in such a way. I love you. Please do not be lost. I give My blessing of mercy to you and to your loved ones.

Notes & Reflections:

NOVEMBER 12, 1992
MESSAGE FROM OUR LADY

My dear little children, learn to rely on God and not on yourself. He leads you towards the fullness of life, bringing freedom of spirit, peace and insight. You will have far greater joy if you are detached from this world's created realities. An unselfish heart knows this and has a pure love for others. The more you love one another, the more God is loved. Have a generous heart, a pure one, and take courage in facing life and its demands. You will find joy with a pure heart and enjoy life, both human and divine, because you will be relying on God, not yourselves. You will find joy in all that there is. I bless you, my little ones, and thank you for responding to my call.

Notes & Reflections:

NOVEMBER 12, 1992
MESSAGE FROM OUR LORD

My dear ones, I am with you again this night as a grace from My Father, to remind you again that even in your trials and in your suffering you are not alone. You, my dear ones, who are giving your hearts to My Father and your Father, are so often ridiculed. Know, my dear ones, that when this happens you are not alone. I hold you, I am with you. I see your struggles and this night I give you My courage. Know that they will not last forever.

You are dear, so dear to My heart. I, your Lord, thank you for truly following Me. You will never be lost as you take My hand. I bless you with My mercy and My peace, and I give you this night My strength in the face of all adversity. You are now living already the Kingdom of God within your heart.

Notes & Reflections:

NOVEMBER 19, 1992
MESSAGE FROM OUR LADY

My dear children, Pray, Pray, Pray! There is still much healing that needs to take place in your hearts and souls. By prayer and listening to the words of my Son can your hurts be transformed into love. Oh children, you too can heal one another by reaching out in love. Reach out, my little ones, in love to the anger and hurts of your brothers and sisters. Then will you find peace in your world. I love you, my little ones, and I'm praying with you always.

Notes & Reflections:

NOVEMBER 19, 1992
MESSAGE FROM OUR LORD

My dear ones, this is the time of your visitation. My Father is allowing Me to again be so present to you. My mother is always with you. My dear ones, this night I come to remind you of how close we are to you. You only need to open your heart -- we are there! We are as close to you as your breath. We surround you with Our love and with Our protection. Feel Our presence with you, around you, within you. You have nothing to fear. Hold on to Us. Our love is with you -- the love of My mother and My love, which is a reflection of the love of God Our Father for you. Peace, my dear ones. Do not be afraid. We are with you! WE ARE WITH YOU!

Notes & Reflections:

DECEMBER 3, 1992
MESSAGE FROM OUR LADY

My dear children, I am your mother who loves you, and I am here because of my Son. I thank you for your commitment to prayer in remaining faithful to my Son's request. My little ones, conversion takes time, and my Son is so very patient. Be at peace to know He is with you, guiding you, and know His hand is so gently upon you. God, in His mercy, is so good and loves you abundantly. Do all that you can to focus on Him, surrendering daily to His will. Be at peace but never cease praying. The Lord is pleased with your prayer because you bring to Him in prayer so many special loved ones. God needs your prayers, your surrendering and openness.

I celebrate with you in prayer for your dedication and faithful commitment. Please unite with me for all those who choose not to follow His way. I need your prayers, my little ones, and there are so many special people searching and so confused. Join me in my quest for unity and happiness for all. I bless you and thank you for responding to my call.

Notes & Reflections:

DECEMBER 3, 1992
MESSAGE FROM OUR LORD

My dear ones, I come to you this night to thank you for listening and for responding to the request of My mother, which is My request also for prayer. Thank you for your faithfulness. My dear ones, in the eyes of the world it is an accomplishment to pray as you have prayed for these five years but, my dear ones, it truly is such a small amount of time. But even with this small amount of time what your prayers are accomplishing is beyond the scope of your world. Know that your prayer matters. Continue to pray.

I see you. I love you, and again this night My mother and I bring you to the throne of My Father. In gratitude, I bless you with My mercy and with My peace, and with the gift of perseverance from the Holy Spirit. Pray as you have been praying and know that your prayers are being answered.

Notes & Reflections:

DECEMBER 10, 1992
MESSAGE FROM OUR LADY

My dear children, this night I come in the name of my Son to bestow upon you special blessings for your commitment in prayer to Him. I thank you, my dear little ones. I know how much you suffer; but I ask that you offer your suffering to my Son and rejoice in your living faith of His truth. My dear children, please continue to pray and to unite here in this place of my Son's divine mercy. Be supportive of my priests and my Son's Church, be obedient to Our Pope, and know they have suffered also very much for my Son. Please pray for the

Church to prevent division. Love and mercy cannot exist where there is division. I love you, my little children, and thank you for responding to my call.
Notes & Reflections:

DECEMBER 10, 1992
MESSAGE FROM OUR LORD

My dear ones, this is indeed the time of My Father's mercy for you. He sends Me. He allows Me to be with you in this way, to call you again to Him. I am now with you. My Father wishes you to believe that you are not alone. In this time My Father gives you many graces.

My dear ones, I ask you this night to accept these graces from Him -- joy, hope, perseverance, and compassion. If you accept these graces, these gifts, My Father will be able to touch so many through you. Do not focus on your failings but upon God's mercy, upon My love for you. I give you the blessing of My mercy this night and the encouragement of Our Holy Spirit to continue listening as I speak continually to your heart. I give you also this night My peace.
Notes & Reflections:

DECEMBER 17, 1992
MESSAGE FROM OUR LADY

My dear little children, during this season I wish to celebrate with you my joy. The greatest gift I have for you is the gift of my Son, your Jesus. My dear little ones, on this night your sufferings will be lifted to my Son and will rest in His most Sacred Heart. You, my little ones, can experience the joy of my Son, a Christmas day, everyday, if you unite and seek Him only. Oh, the joy of Him who reigns in the world. He is your peace and comfort. No gift is greater than my Son. I love you, my little ones, and I share with you my most precious love -- my Son.

Pray and prepare, for this time is a time of grace. Put aside all anxieties and stressful circumstances and see my Son there in your midst. Focus on Him, tend to Him and rejoice! I love you and I celebrate with you your five years. Bless you and thank you for your response to my call.
Notes & Reflections:

DECEMBER 17, 1992
MESSAGE FROM OUR LORD

My dear ones, as you again, in a very few days, celebrate My birth, My Father again sends Me to you. I have been called by many titles, but the one I encourage you to embrace is Emmanuel -- God with you. I am that gift given to you by God, My Father. I am always with you. From that moment that I was given life through My mother, Mary -- Emmanuel, God with you. You are not alone. I, the Son of God, am always with you. The gift, a gift from God -- the God who loves you. That love is poured out on you through Me, through My birth, through My life, through My death, and through My resurrection. I am your gift from God. And so this night I, the gift from God, give you, each of you, My peace, My strength; and I assure you again of My continuing presence, my real presence with you! I love you. I am with you. I am EMMANUEL!

Notes & Reflections:

JANUARY 7, 1993
MESSAGE FROM OUR LADY

My dear little children, praised be Jesus. I rejoice in Him for allowing me to be here with you. My dear ones, I wish for you only to focus on my Son, and seek His acceptance first and not of others. My little ones, only Jesus has a plan so beautiful and pure in His faithfulness for you. Do not be distracted by the words of others, but look to God to fulfill you and guide you. You all need each other, but only in Jesus can His plans be fulfilled in each of you. Jesus has a great plan of love and peace and freedom for all of you. Look to His love. Surrender and love Him. I love you, my little ones, but I urge you to be so secure in my Son that the words of others will not take you from that what my Son has planned for you. In Him all of you will be united in harmony and love. Praise be Jesus, my little ones. Pray! Pray! Pray to my Son.

I bless you and thank you for responding to my call. Serve God first and then you will be able to serve each other.

Notes & Reflections:

JANUARY 14, 1993
MESSAGE FROM OUR LADY

My dear little children, in these times of struggle and economic disasters, I wish you to know of the great love my Son and I have for you. My little ones, procure your relationship with God now. Do not wait. I am confident in my Son that here, at the center of His Divine Mercy, His people will be strong in faithfulness to Him. Faith in God is the only means to salvation and prayer is the way to purity and holiness. Only God can merit you with this grace, but your surrender to Him is the gateway to your total joy and protection.

Pray with me, my little ones. I need desperately your prayers for peace in this world. I love you and bless you in the name of He Who has sent me. Thank you for responding to my call and the call of my Son. Peace.

Notes & Reflections:

JANUARY 14, 1993
MESSAGE FROM OUR LORD

My dear ones, I ask you this night to truly listen and to trust Me, Who gave My life for you, and for Whom I was raised up by My Father. You trust Me only partially. My dear ones, if you still keep the control of your life, you block My will for you. Trusting means giving up to God all of who you are. When you trust then you will be able to listen. When you do not trust you are afraid to listen because you are afraid of what I may ask you. Trust Me when I say I wish only good for you. I am with you. I invite you again to begin anew -- to trust. Trust so that you may truly listen; and, as you listen, you will indeed hear Me. I love you, and I bless you this night with My mercy and with My peace.
Notes & Reflections:

JANUARY 21, 1993
MESSAGE FROM OUR LADY

My dear little children, I am your mother of God here to tell you that the greatest love story is contained in the Sacred Host. When you receive your Jesus, open your hearts and your minds in purity allowing my Son to permeate every cell in your being.

I love you, my dear ones, but only through trust and love can you grow in holiness. Only in my Son can you grow in holiness. Only He can merit you with the graces of love and trust. Faith is a gift to you. Please pray and never lose faith. No matter what devastations are in the world - never lose faith. Trust my Jesus, trust your Jesus. He is yours. Bless you, my little ones. Thank you for responding to my call.
Notes & Reflections:

JANUARY 21, 1993
MESSAGE FROM OUR LORD

My dear ones, I come this night to remind you once again that I am with you and that I love you. I see your hearts. I see that you wish to give them to Me but I also see fear, and wondering, and questioning. My dear ones, please know that I love you beyond what you can ever grasp, and that I cherish each of you and bring you to My Father. I tell you, hold on. I give you this night the grace of My perseverance. I encourage you not to give up, not to look at yourself, but to look at Me. Everything will be alright. There is no need to worry. I am with you. I am walking with you these days. Peace I give to you. Peace!
Notes & Reflections:

JANUARY 28, 1993
MESSAGE FROM OUR LADY

My dear children, I am your mother who comes to be with you this night. Oh my dear ones, I see your struggles and I ask you this night to pray for peace in your hearts. Pray to be able to accept change in your life. I ask you to pray for acceptance in the will of God in your life. I am always with you. I love you, my dear little ones. Peace to you!
Notes & Reflections:

JANUARY 28, 1993
MESSAGE FROM OUR LORD

My dear ones, I come to you this night to ask you not to try to understand the will of My Father in your life, but simply to trust. I know, my dear ones, how incredibly hard that must seem to you for I, your Lord, in My humanness was tempted, also. But I ask you to follow the example that I gave and to trust. I am walking with you so there truly is nothing to fear. This night I call you to trust and I, your Lord, see that so often in your attempt to understand you leave the will of My Father and begin to interpret what you think is His will. Come to Me as I am with you in My most Blessed Sacrament, and trust. You are so close. Don't give up. You will see why I called you to trust. This night I give you my courage. Hold on to Me within your heart. All will be well. I tell you all is well within you even now!
Notes & Reflections:

FEBRUARY 4, 1993
MESSAGE FROM OUR LADY

My dear little children, I am here with you because of my Son's great love and mercy. I will continue to be with you as you continue to give of yourselves to your family and your brethren. My little ones, if you feel nothing, are alone or feel abandoned, know that it is in your nothingness that you are everything in my Son. It is in your ordinariness that you are extraordinary.

My little ones, please trust in my Son. Be simple, loving and kind disciples of my Son. Focus on Him. Pray! Use the sacrament of reconciliation, fast and give to my Son what He has given to you. He loves you. He needs you. I need you. I love you and am here to unite all in His love. Bless you, my little ones. Bless you. Thank you for responding to this call. Focus on Him. Fight the evil one with love of yourself, your family and brothers and sisters. Fight with love and forgiveness. Peace!
Notes & Reflections:

FEBRUARY 4, 1993
MESSAGE FROM OUR LORD

My dear ones, I am with you always. In each step of your journey I am there. I speak to you this night of My Father, who is also your Father. My dear ones, He is not a wrathful God. How could a wrathful God love you so much as to send you His only Son to save you. Would a wrathful God send you His Holy Spirit who will always be with you? My Father loves you.

I am here again with you this night to say to you one more time -- God does not want to be distant from you. My dear ones, he sends Me to you. I am with you. Look at Me! See Me within your hearts. I give you My peace. I give you My healing. There is no need of fear. Look at Me! I am your light! I am your safety! I am the Son of God for you, given to you. Be at peace! Be at peace!
Notes & Reflections:

FEBRUARY 11, 1993
MESSAGE FROM OUR LADY

My dear little children, I love you and come in the name of Jesus. Praise Jesus. Praise my Son, my little ones. I once again wish to say to you that if you cannot truly trust unconditionally in my Son, then you cannot truly believe that God exists. It is through my Son that all joy, peace, harmony and the virtue of love can exist. My little ones, if you love you will trust, hope and endure. Please, my little ones, God loves you, and through His Sacred Heart will you grow in holiness. TRUST HIM! Take the risk you see it as and step out into His arms. He is there to guide you. Do not be afraid to give yourself unconditionally to my Son. Do not be afraid. You will be secure and live in joy and tranquility. Bless you, my dear ones. Thank you for responding to my call.
Notes & Reflections:

FEBRUARY 11, 1993
MESSAGE FROM OUR LORD

My dear ones, you are children of My Father. He has not abandoned you. He sends Me to you and My mother to remind you of the great gift in the inheritance which is yours. My dear ones, so often through fear you live as orphans and as a homeless person, not knowing where you belong. Again I remind you, you are children of God and your home is with Him no matter how difficult the journey. Know that this is just the journey, not your home. You were created and are still being created in the image of My Father, of Myself and of Our Holy Spirit. My dear ones, this creating requires time as you look upon it. Look with My Father. He is instantaneous.

This night I give you My strength for the journey. My peace I give you. I and My mother are with you each step of your journey. Persevere! We are with you!
Notes & Reflections:

FEBRUARY 18, 1993
MESSAGE FROM OUR LADY

My dear little children, I love you and come always in the name of my Son. Praise be Jesus. Look to Him, my little ones. It is so important that you always look first to my Son to grace you. He is the one who loves you to grace you with His virtues. My little ones, His way may not initially be your way but, if you surrender to Him and trust Him, then you will be able to trust others. First look to God. Procure your relationship with God first; and then you will have the blessings to love unconditionally, and to trust one another. I present to you my Son. Receive Him. Hope in Him and always look to Him for guidance in the midst of your confusion. I bless you, my little ones, in the name of my Son. Thank you, my little ones, for responding to my call.
Notes & Reflections:

MARCH 4, 1993
MESSAGE FROM OUR LADY

My dear little children, praise be Jesus! My little ones, remember that you belong to Jesus and, if you plunge yourselves into His heart, you will be awakened to a renewed way of living. Put aside your distractions and know you belong to Him. Do not be frustrated or discouraged. No matter what happens, you have my Son. Only in my Son can you live in peace and in love during these difficult times. Be at peace and joy-filled little children knowing He is here with you and will never leave you because you belong to Him. Bless you, my little ones, and thank you for responding to my call.
Notes & Reflections:

MARCH 11, 1993
MESSAGE FROM OUR LADY

My dear children, I come to bring tidings of peace. I am your mother who loves you. My Son loves you, my little ones. Please focus on Him. Take the time to be with my Son in His Eucharistic presence. He enthusiastically awaits you. Look to Him for acceptance and understanding before looking to one another in times of struggle. My little ones, only Jesus has the power, wisdom and knowledge to help you. He will bless you with abundant graces if you simply surrender and love Him.

My dear, dear children, I ask you again to put aside your trivial misunderstandings which are

preventing you from focusing on my Son. Make straight your way of love through my Son. Only He can lead you in the true way of love. Thank you for responding to my call.
Notes & Reflections:

MARCH 18, 1993
MESSAGE FROM OUR LADY

My dear children, I am your mother who comes to be with you this night. I wrap you in my mantle of love. Children, your journey to my Son is by *faith,* not by sight. Continue to walk in your blindness, but know my Son and I are here with you walking every step. My Son is leading you, my little ones! Be patient in your blindness. Be patient in your trials. LOVE! My dear ones, pray with all your hearts. I love you! Peace to you!
Notes & Reflections:

MARCH 18, 1993
MESSAGE FROM OUR LORD

My dear ones, I come this night to remind you of how much My Father loves you. He sends Me this night to ask again for your faithfulness. My dear ones, you are faithful! I give you My strength this night to continue on your faithful journey back to My Father. You do listen to My voice. How thankful I am to you! You are at last listening to Me! As you listen, I will continue to speak to each of you and to all of you. Listen with your whole being. Through your faithfulness I will be able to touch many. Please continue to be faithful no matter what anyone else says or does. Listen to Me. Come to Me and I will give you rest, and strength, and peace. I bless you, my faithful ones. I love you!
Notes & Reflections:

MARCH 25, 1993
MESSAGE FROM OUR LORD

My dear ones, this night I come to remind you of what a gift I have given you in My mother. She is the sign -- the sign of trust, the sign of obedience, the sign of humility. She is the sign of all times reminding everyone of who God is! My dear ones, I ask you to cherish her, to cherish her presence with you. She loves you as do I. Follow her humility, follow her obedience, follow her trust, and she will lead you back to Me. Honor her as I honor her, and know that I love her as she loves Me. This night, in her honor, I bless you with My mercy, My peace!
Notes & Reflections:

APRIL 1, 1993
MESSAGE FROM OUR LADY

My dear little children, I am your mother, so full of grace. I tell you this night grace is being poured out to all my children. I ask you at this time to allow yourself to walk in a silent journey with my Jesus. Allow Him to bring you so close to His heart. Offer to Him all your joys and all your sufferings as you walk silently with my beloved Jesus. I love you, my little ones, and I bless you.
Notes & Reflections:

APRIL 1, 1993
MESSAGE FROM OUR LORD

My dear ones, again this night I come to ask that you trust in Me and in the will of My Father Who has sent Me. My dear ones, so much you try to understand My will and the will of My Father. It would be better if you would try as hard to trust in Me. The closer you come the more it seems you become distracted trying to understand. If you do not trust you will never understand. My dear ones, what My Father has for you is beyond anything you could ever imagine. Please believe Me when I say you need to trust in God. I love you. Trust in God. Trust this night in what I say to you.
Notes & Reflections:

APRIL 22, 1993
MESSAGE FROM OUR LORD

My dear ones, I, your Risen Lord, am here this night to remind you again that I am with you; that I walk with you; that I live in My Spirit within you; that you are never alone or away from Me. My dear ones, I give you My life. I call you this night to accept the love and the mercy and the compassion that God, My Father, and your Father, offers you through Me.

I encourage you -- listen to Our Holy Spirit speaking to your heart. Take courage, be strong! Even in your weakness your strength is the strength that I give you. Stand in My light and be that light, My light to those around you. Live My truth and My joy, and allow My peace to flow through you to others. I bless you this night with My healing mercy. Rejoice, my dear ones, for because of My Father's love I have conquered even death, not only for Myself but for you. I love you. My peace is with you.
Notes & Reflections:

MAY 6, 1993
MESSAGE FROM OUR LORD

My dear ones, this night I invite you agai to come to Me and to open your hearts so that I may come to you. I ask you to bring to Me each day all of those things that are part of your

suffering and part of your joy. Offer them to Me so that I may take them to the Father, your Father and My Father. Give them to Me so that you do not have to carry them alone. My dear ones, you tire yourselves! Allow Me to strengthen you and to renew you, but for this you must come to Me. I love you and I wish to heal you, and forgive you, and strengthen you. Know that My Father has sent Me to be with you -- and I am! This night I bless you again with My mercy and My peace.
Notes & Reflections:

MAY 13, 1993
MESSAGE FROM OUR LADY

My dear little children, praise be Jesus! My dear ones, the Mass is the greatest prayer. Humble yourselves before my Son in the Mass and He will make you perfect. He will give to you all which you need to make you righteous in Him. My little ones, Satan is trying to destroy families and is very aggressive now against the youth. Pray, Pray, Pray! He knows his time is soon over and he is trying desperately to gather all and destroy your happiness. Pray and love one another. Love, please! I implore you to conversion and prayer now. I need your prayers. My Son is merciful. He is MERCY. He is LOVE. Bless you, my little ones. I take your petitions to my Son. Come, my little ones. Please return back to my Son through the sacraments and pray for the youth. Thank you for responding to my call.
Notes & Reflections:

MAY 13, 1993
MESSAGE FROM OUR LORD

My dear ones, I come to you this night to tell you once again that I give you, I offer you, My mercy. As you accept My mercy, you will experience living in the love of My Father with Me. I offer you also this night the gift of My joy, the joy that is also My mother's joy. There is only one way to live in this joy that I offer, the joy in which My mother lives, and it is to keep the commandments of My Father as My mother did, as I did. This is truly, my dear ones, the source of joy. You know this already. It is truly simple, but I know also it is very difficult. I give you then, because of this difficulty, My strength this night to overcome the evil one, the strength of My Spirit which banishes him forever. Accept this tonight and, through this strength, My mercy will flow, My love will be in your heart and you will be surrounded in joy. Know that I am with you always. There is nothing to fear; and My mother will lead you, if you allow her, to Me, and together she and I will present you to God Our Father. I love you! I LOVE YOU!
Notes & Reflections:

MAY 20, 1993
MESSAGE FROM OUR LADY

My dear children, praise be Jesus. My dear little ones, pray that you will be intimate with Jesus with a deep living faith that will bring you into His sweetness of love which surpasses all knowledge. My Son loves you, my children, and wishes for you to love one another unconditionally, without reservations and without judgment. Please, my little ones, love and allow yourself to be loved. Do not allow Satan to disrupt your focus. Please, I need you and I need you to look beyond to His love, removing yourselves from your own self-interests. He will give you abundant graces and heal your wounds with His tender love. Bless you, my little ones, for responding to my call.

Notes & Reflections:

MAY 20, 1993
MESSAGE FROM OUR LORD

My dear ones, as Heaven and earth celebrate this feast of My ascension into Heaven, I am with you this night to remind you that I am always with you, that I do keep my promise, that I am here. My dear ones, just as My disciples did not understand what I said to them, I see you also not understanding. I know, My dear ones, it is so very difficult for you to trust in what I say because, for you, My will seems to take such a long time. My dear ones, look upon My disciples and see how I fulfilled what I said to them. I gave them My spirit, Our Spirit, the Spirit of My Father and Me, the same Spirit We have given to you. Use this day as an encouragement to you to be faithful and to trust in Me. I am with you now, and always and I am coming again. I give you this night the gift of My hope and My perseverance. I love you! I love you! Endure!

Notes & Reflections:

MAY 27, 1993
MESSAGE FROM OUR LADY

My dear little children. Praise be Jesus. My little ones, the true experience is that of your faith. It is given to you from God. Always look to His goodness and live His word. Read the scriptures; study them, and the Holy Spirit will guide you in truth. Never fear because Jesus is your Saviour. But please pray and look to Jesus so He can cleanse you, teach you, guide you and protect you. God awaits your love patiently. Give all of your hearts in prayer to Him. God is living and is everywhere because of His creation of the world. Be at peace, my little children, and prepare in reconciliation and prayer for Pentecost. I bless you in Jesus. Thank you for responding to my call.

Notes & Reflections:

MAY 27, 1993
MESSAGE FROM OUR LORD

My dear ones, I, your Saviour, your Jesus of Mercy, am with you. I come this night to encourage you no matter what the odds or barrier, to live My truth, to speak My truth. Before you can live or speak that truth which is Mine, you need to listen to Me, your Lord, who speaks continually to your heart. Come to Me. Come away with Me and listen. Be refreshed with My truth. Be energized with My very life. I have given you Our Spirit, the Holy Spirit of God; and I, your Lord, bless you this night with My peace. Be joyful, My little ones, as you live and speak the truth for the truth will not only vindicate you but will set you free. Remember I am always with you, always with you!

Notes & Reflections:

JUNE 3, 1993
MESSAGE FROM OUR LADY

My dear little children, praise be Jesus. My little ones, Jesus has graced you abundantly in ways you do not even recognize. Always be grateful and continue to seek Him in His love and tenderness. There are many things that you may not understand and may not even know the changes that my Son is doing in you. Be assured that by trusting in Him that there are many beautiful changes and fruits surfacing in your lives. My little ones, I ask you for unconditional trust and surrender, love and forgiveness and patience. Have hope, my little ones. God is with you. We are here for you because of love for you. Pray little ones. Pray fervently. I bless you in the name of my Jesus of Mercy. Peace to you. Love one another in His peace. Thank you for responding to my call.

Notes & Reflections:

JUNE 3, 1993
MESSAGE FROM OUR LORD

My dear ones, I come in love this night to you to bless those of you who are living the sacred covenant and sacrament of marriage. Know, my dear ones who My Father has called to live this life, that I am with you. Take courage and be strengthened by My love this night. Know that in living the sacrament, I am with you; in your patient endurance of trials, I am with you; in the joy of each other and of your family, I am with you. Know that you are a sign of God's hope for this world. Take courage, My dear ones, for a call to live this life of selfless love that nothing goes unnoticed by My Father. Nothing is so small of your self-sacrifice that is not worth much in the Kingdom of My Father. I thank you this night for responding in love to this call. I bless each of you and your families. Know that I am always with you.

Notes & Reflections:

JUNE 10, 1993
MESSAGE FROM OUR LADY

My dear little children, praise be Jesus. My little ones, know that not all relationships are easy to deal with. But if Jesus is in your heart there will be love. My Son has so many graces which He wishes to give to you and as you surrender in trust daily, He is able to give to you every source of strength and grace needed to procure a healthy and happy relationship. Be at peace in your daily walk, my little ones, as you give unconditionally to Jesus. He is with you and He will make every fruit blossom in every situation which you think is impossible. Nothing is impossible with God. Your focus, however, must always be on Jesus and your happiness and growth of holiness in Him. I bless you, my little ones, and thank you for responding to my call of patience in relationships with love being your source of light and peace.

Notes & Reflections:

JUNE 10, 1993
MESSAGE FROM OUR LORD

My dear ones, I come to you this night to remind you of the gift of freedom that you have been given through Our Holy Spirit. This freedom, My dear ones, freedom in the Lord is a gift truly which sets your spirit free. This freedom comes from obedience to My Father and to yours. My dear ones, I know how difficult it is sometimes to be obedient when this world in which you live is so disobedient to My Father and to yours. But know that as you are obedient you will experience more of the freedom of God. I love you, My dear ones. I encourage you in your obedience; and I offer My mother and Myself as your examples of obedience. This obedience will lead you through suffering and dying to the freedom of new life. Know that I am with you in your journey of obedience for I have gone before you in that same journey. My blessing to you this night gives you strength.

Notes & Reflections:

JUNE 17, 1993
MESSAGE FROM OUR LADY

My dear little children, praise be Jesus! My little ones, as many of you leave to return to your homes know that I leave with you. And to you my little ones who remain, I remain with you here. I am your Mother of Joy. I am the same mother who was and who is. I am your mother. As my Son is your Jesus Who was and Who is, He also is here with you, to be with you always no matter where you are. He remains with you. He is your Jesus of Mercy. My little, little children, know that your prayers are so much needed because of the power of salvation which frees many souls. Never cease praying. Always unite in love and unity daily. MY JESUS AWAITS YOUR PRAYERS AND YOUR LOVE. NEVER FORGET HOW MUCH YOU ARE LOVED. I thank you, my children, for taking seriously my call to prayer and unity. Pray

daily with all your heart and do not fear. I AM HERE AND I AM HERE AS MY SON IS HERE. HE IS MERCY AND LOVE. Bless you, my little ones, and thank you for responding to my call. Peace.
Notes & Reflections:

JUNE 17, 1993
MESSAGE FROM OUR LORD

My dear ones, I come this night to reassure you that I do listen to what you say to Me. Through all of the words of your mouth I look first into your heart. My dear ones, never fear to ask, never fear to speak because through your words you will eventually give Me your heart. I tell you again I do listen. I do hear every word, and I present you each time you pray to My heavenly Father. I love you! Know that I love you. Your prayers do not go unanswered because they do not go unlistened to. My Father answers your prayers within your heart. Listen with your heart and you will hear us speak to you. We speak to your heart in peace and in mercy. I love you! I listen! We answer!
Notes & Reflections:

JUNE 24, 1993
MESSAGE FROM OUR LADY

My dear ones, I come this night to encourage you to follow the example of John. Be courageous speaking and living the truth no matter what the cost. John preceded my Son. He spoke the truth, he lived the truth, and in that he was joy filled and proclaimed the glory of God. Follow the example of John. Allow my Son to increase within you, allow Him to be your all. I love you, my dear ones, my dear little ones. I give you my love this night and I bless you and take your hearts with mine to the heart of my Son. We are always with you as you live the truth, as you speak the truth, as my Son increases within you.
Notes & Reflections:

JULY 15, 1993
MESSAGE FROM OUR LORD

My dear ones, I invite you again this night to truly come to Me with all of your heart. Come to Me in My word; come to Me in the Eucharist of My love; come to Me in the quiet of your heart. As you do, I will comfort you; I will give you peace; I will heal you. Come! Do not wait. Come! I love you. Come to Me! I will never disappoint you. Come to Me so that My mercy may be poured out upon you. It is I, My dear ones, who has been sent by My Father to refresh you, to encourage you, to save you. But you need to come to Me. I am with you. Do not be distracted or led astray. Come! I bless you and give you the grace of My healing this night. I speak to your heart My word of love.
Notes & Reflections:

JULY 22, 1993
MESSAGE FROM OUR LORD

My dear ones, I, your Lord, invite you this night to come to Me so that I may make you into a new person. Bring Me all of your failings, all of your sins - your sins for which I died; for I wish to heal you, and forgive you, and restore your innocence. My dear ones, do not hold on to your sins. Hold on to Me! Allow Me to make you into a new creation as I present you to My Father who is your Father. I love you, My dear ones. Come to Me and I will restore your innocence. I bless you this night with My mercy, and My healing, and My grace.

Notes & Reflections:

JULY 29, 1993
MESSAGE FROM OUR LORD

My dear ones, My Father and I and Our Holy Spirit have been with you from the very beginning. My Father sends Me now again to you to remind you that We are still with you, Father, Son and Spirit. This night I invite you to be with Us, to be conscious of Us with you every moment of every day. It saddens My heart, My dear ones, when I see you acting as if you were alone, as if you were orphans. Be with Us in thought, and in action; in attitude and in spirit. The strength that My Father will give you, the grace that comes from Our Spirit and the mercy that I long to give you is waiting for you. Accept these gifts and live in unity with Us. I love you. I am still with you. My Father is with you and Our Spirit abides within you. I bless you this night with My real presence. Peace.

Notes & Reflections:

AUGUST 5, 1993
MESSAGE FROM OUR LADY

My dear little ones, I, your mother, come to you this night to invite you to look again at my Son, Jesus. To follow Him truly is to take up your cross, to sacrifice, and to suffer whatever comes as you follow Him. Little ones, so many times it is tempting to separate the cross from your life. Separating the cross from your life is separating yourself from my Son. Know that He is with you in your suffering. He is with you as you carry your cross, and it is only through your cross that you will reach Heaven. Remember this, little ones, when you face each day what my Son asks of you. Know that He has sent me to you. Know that I am with you, that I pray with you and for you. I love you and I take you in my arms and present you to my Son. Do not be afraid of the cross, my dear little ones. It is the sign of your victory because it is the sign of my Son's victory. Live in His peace and know that I love you.

Notes & Reflections:

SEPTEMBER 2, 1993
MESSAGE FROM OUR LORD

My dear ones, I come this night to remind you that I, your Lord, am always with you. I ask you again to trust in Me and in My Father Who is your Father. Trust, My dear ones, especially in those times when the situations in your life seem impossible or overpowering, I am with you. I will never abandon you. As you trust you allow Me to bring more of the gifts that I wish to give. This night, My dear ones, I again bless you with My spirit, with peace and with courage, with healing and with My mercy. Trust, trust! I am with you.

Notes & Reflections:

SEPTEMBER 9, 1993
MESSAGE FROM OUR LADY

My dear little ones, I come this night to encourage you to listen to my Son. Know that forgiveness and love go hand-in-hand. Know also that these are very difficult to live. My Son calls us to the narrow way; to the way of His light and His truth; to the way which truly will cause suffering to us, not because of what He asks but because of the resistance of the world. When you are loving and forgiving then you are full of my Son's peace. The world does not understand and there are those in the world who will hate you for loving, for living a life of forgiveness. I am with you through this each step of your way. My dear, dear little ones, know that my Son, our Lord Jesus, truly is your way and my way to God Our Father. In His name this night I bless you. Know that we love you and although His way is narrow and sometimes difficult, you are not alone. Be at peace my dear children. I am your mother!

Notes & Reflections:

SEPTEMBER 16, 1993
MESSAGE FROM OUR LADY

Praise be my Son, Jesus, your Saviour. O my little ones, the grace of God is upon you. My dear, dear children, I need your prayers. I need your prayers desperately for peace in this world; for the salvation of mankind through love and kindness. These days, my little ones, there is so much evil. Satan does not want those that are with him, but he wants those who wish to follow the way of my Son. He wishes to molest them. He wishes to cause great devastation through destruction and division. Days of great division are coming, days in which many in the world will choose not to walk with my Son.

I wish for all to return back to God. Little ones, please unite in prayer, in harmony and in love. Through kindness and through love you will conquer the world; for my Son has conquered the world. My Son is with you.

My little ones, I love you and I know you can love, love far beyond the surface, love deep to the core. Be strong, take courage, courage in Jesus. Look into your heart and rest in my Son. Know I am with you. Know my Son loves you tremendously and it is because of Him you ARE. Try, my little ones, you must try. Fight with all your being to return back to the good ways, the simple ways, the loving ways. Love one another and then my Son will know how deeply you love Him. Bless you, my little ones, and thank you for responding to my call. Peace.

Notes & Reflections:

SEPTEMBER 23, 1993
MESSAGE FROM OUR LADY

My dear little children, praise be Jesus! My little ones, never be afraid. Do not fear. My Son is with you always. Live in simplicity and love. Pray for peace and love to dwell in your hearts at all times. Pray to be adopted by those in Heaven to intercede for you through peace and through love. You are little children, and you are very much loved by my Son and many. Do not fear for what is now happening in your lives, but look to the true happiness of your TRUE life in eternal bliss, and be at peace through love.

God has His hand upon you. He has graced you. Return to simple ways of thoughts, prayers and actions, and you will live in His peace of His love. You are so special, my little ones. It is the evil one trying to cause confusion and division. Remember, Jesus is gentle and tender and kind, AND YOU ARE HIS. HE LOVES YOU AND WILL NEVER FORGET YOU, even though others may forget you. He is your hope, your ONLY hope. Return back to Him. Bless you, my little ones. Thank you for responding to my call.

Notes & Reflections:

SEPTEMBER 23, 1993
MESSAGE FROM OUR LORD

I invite you to go deep within your heart, and there to listen to Me speaking to you. There in the innermost recesses of your heart you will find and discover who I AM for you, and what I want for you. Each of you is precious to Me. I love you. It is My desire to grace you from your innermost being, so that you may truly be free as the sons and daughters of My Father. Pray, My dear ones, to enter into your heart. I dwell there because of Our Holy Spirit. Be at peace. I give you again this night My peace, My strength. Know that I am with you. Allow Me to truly be your Lord.

Notes & Reflections:

SEPTEMBER 30, 1993
MESSAGE FROM OUR LADY

My dear little children, praise be Jesus! My little ones, put aside all worries and anxieties, and give your love totally to My Son. Love Him. He wants all of you. Ask Him to remove your wandering thoughts and doubts, so that you can give yourself totally to Him. Simply love Him, praise Him, and just be with Him. He awaits your love. He desires you.

Please, my little ones, there is much devastation in this world, and it is very important that you tend to Jesus. Accept His will and trust in His goodness. Do not allow the evil one or his companions to torture you interiorly. Be free in my Son by putting aside any anxiousness, and love Him. He will grant you His peace. Call on your angels for assistance. I bless you, my little ones. Thank you for responding to my call.

Notes & Reflections:

OCTOBER 7, 1993
MESSAGE FROM OUR LADY

My dear little children, praise be Jesus! This night, my little ones, I want you to know that freedom can only come by living the truth. Know, my children, that the way you live, your moral values, and your love will be the deciding factor to being free. Live the truth of God set by His word, His commandments. Be free interiorly and exteriorly. Be obedient to my most beloved Pope. Do not turn from him. He has outlined the way to freedom. He has outlined the truth. I love you, my little ones; and I come to tell you that many of your moral values are not the way of truth, the way of my Son. To be free you must live in His truth.

Please pray the rosary. Many graces come from the rosary and with my Son's grace you will be guided to live in His truth, and you will be protected. My Son will grace you in changing to live His goodness, if you are willing and open to knowing the truth. The truth will challenge you and lead you to freedom, peace, happiness and holiness. Bless you, my little ones, and thank you for responding to my call.

Notes & Reflections:

OCTOBER 7, 1993
MESSAGE FROM OUR LORD

My dear little ones, so often I see that you ask but then also you tell Me what to give you. So often I see you seeking, but then again you tell Me what you are looking for. So often you knock, but only on the door that you already know. My dear ones, I have told you only to ask, to seek, and to knock. Allow My Father and yours to give what He sees is best for you. I love you. And so often I see you not allowing My Father to give what he wants. My narrow minded children, do you think that God is as limited as you? I am here this night to ask you not to limit the power of God in your life. He would do so much more for you and through you if you would allow it.

My dear ones, listen to me this night - change your attitude and, if need be, even the way of your prayer. You constantly are looking for freedom. I, your Jesus, ask you to give God, My Father, and your Father, freedom to act in your life as He wants to. Then you will truly be free; you will truly be joyful; you will truly be peaceful; and then will your prayers truly be answered. I give you My peace and My mercy this night. I bless you and love you.

Notes & Reflections:

OCTOBER 14, 1993
MESSAGE FROM OUR LADY

My dear little children, praise be Jesus! My little ones, please do not despair. Have hope and live in faith and in my Son's love, and in His fidelity. Please my little ones, focus on prayer and practice my Son's words through love. Pray; rejoice in His greatest gift in the Mass; study His word and be committed to following His way. It is time to remain faithful to your commitments of prayer. Do not replace your prayer time with other options. There is only one priceless option - that of your desire to pray and to be with my Son. He will grace you, my little ones, with abundant virtues if you remain committed to Him, allowing Him to challenge you to growth. I love you, my little ones, and bless you in His name. Please take the time for prayer and study His word. Do not lose sight of your focus on Him. Thank you for responding to my call, a priceless calling to prayer and love.

Notes & Reflections:

OCTOBER 14, 1993
MESSAGE FROM OUR LORD

My dear ones, I come this night from My Father who sends Me to remind you again of His love. He has shown you His love through Me, through My life, through My death, and as I was raised up by Him, through My resurrection. Now he sends Me again. And again I willingly come to encourage you to listen more closely to what God is saying to you, what My Father has said through Me - keep His commandments as I kept His commandments. Be faithful to Him. My dear ones, persevere on your journey. Do not allow fatigue to overcome you. Know that I am with you. I know it is not easy, but with Me each step can be filled with joy. Listening and faithfulness will strengthen you as you continue. Bless you with the mercy of My heart and the love of My Father, Who is your Father. Amen!

Notes & Reflections:

OCTOBER 28, 1993
MESSAGE FROM OUR LADY

My dear little children, praise be Jesus! My little ones, know that Jesus in His infinite mercy is gently molding you. When you struggle with interior pain, it is difficult to realize how gracious Jesus is in allowing the many things of yourself to surface. It is because of His love that He promotes healing through your pain. Self-abandonment and detachment are necessary but are also unending struggles for you. Know, my little ones that spiritual freedom can surface from your struggles. It is your purity of intention and your openness that will allow divine providence to victoriously ensue. Continue to pray, my little ones, and allow God's will to be done. Do not fight interior cleansing. In order to live in union with Him you must die on one level only to be reborn on another.

I bless you, my little ones. I am with you and love you. God loves you. Do not fight His love by trying to control. Rest in Him. Be at peace. Do not keep your distance. Jesus loves you. Thank you for responding to my call.

Notes & Reflections:

OCTOBER 28, 1993
MESSAGE FROM OUR LORD

My dear ones, as I called My apostles I am calling you this day at this time. As I called each of them from their different and varied works and labors and lives, I call you, all of you, who are children of My Father, from your varied and different works and labors and ways of lives. But there is a difference, My dear ones, I call you not to come out of your different ways of lives, not to leave your different tasks or labors, but rather to stay where you are and to work and labor, showing those around you that God is the center of your life. This is the way My Father and I, and Our Holy Spirit will touch and transform the lives of many. You will not be alone for I will be with you. Our Spirit will be guiding you. I encourage you to use the gifts that My Father has given to you where you are at this moment to touch those around you. This is the kind of apostle I call you to be. I love you and I bless you this night with My strength and My courage, My mercy and My peace.

Notes & Reflections:

NOVEMBER 4, 1993
MESSAGE FROM OUR LADY

My dear little children, praise be Jesus! My little ones, I am your Lady of Joy. I bring you tidings of love and peace. My little, little children, love unconditionally. Strive always to abandon yourself unconditionally to God so that you will be able to love unconditionally. Do not allow self-deceit to pull you away from my Son. Even when you think you are loving in purity as Jesus would have you love, you can fall into loving according to your standards. Love unconditionally. Love all. It is very important that abandonment of yourself be a daily offering to my Son so that you can love in purity, unconditionally, as Jesus would have you love. It is in loving that you are united to the Triune God. Bless you, my little ones. Bless you in the name of Jesus. Peace. Thank you for responding to my call.

Notes & Reflections:

NOVEMBER 4, 1993
MESSAGE FROM OUR LORD

My dear ones, I am with you this night to tell you that you, who are children of God, are judging one another. My dear ones, I ask you - who made you judge over anyone? There is but one judge and that has been given to Me by My Father. My dear ones, do not be self-righteous. Look down on no one. Pray instead for those you are concerned for. I look into your hearts and I see so much judgment, so much selfishness. My dear ones, please do not judge lest you be judged. I give you the grace that you need to pray, not to judge. I give you the grace to be simple humble children of God My Father and yours. Be those children. Love simply. Embrace the truth. As you do these things you will not have time to judge others. I challenge you this night to listen to My words and to put them into practice so that you may give honor and glory to God. I love you and I am with you always. I bless you this night with My peace and with My mercy.

Notes & Reflections:

NOVEMBER 11, 1993
MESSAGE FROM OUR LADY

My dear little children, praise be Jesus! My little ones, remember I have said every prayer which is from the heart is another rose which is given to my Son. My little ones, pray with all your heart. Do not only recite words, but sing with songs of praise every word through your heart. My Son wants your heart, not your words. He wants your actions to speak your words. My Son loves you, my little ones. I wish for all of you to know truly how present I am to you, all of you. My Son has gifted you to allow me to be here with you in this special way. That is why I ask you to take seriously my calling. Tonight I again speak words of unity and harmony.

It is time, my little ones, that you begin to live in unity. There are far too many people living in ways of division and unmerciful means through lack of kindness. Please return back to God. Pray with your heart and He will guide you how to live in unity through loving. Please, please, please love one another. How can I give you new messages if you are not living these existing ones. I need you, my little ones, and I bless you in my Son's name. Blessed be God. Thank you for responding to my call.

Notes & Reflections:

NOVEMBER 18, 1993
MESSAGE FROM OUR LADY

My dear little children, praise be Jesus! My little ones, I come to you as a gift from God in these times of great need in order that you will return back to God. I have come so frequently because little is being paid in attention to my messages. My little ones, please heed my words. I am calling you to great prayer and love and patience. I desire to intercede for you to God imploring His mercy. My Son loves you, my little ones, and all focus should be on Him. Allow me to help you pray and allow me to intercede for you. I ask you this night for your patience. Take the pain of patience in the troubles of your brother. Remember, my little ones, that if you cannot be patient with your own imperfections, how can you expect others to be perfect. Bear with patience all tribulations of yourself and others. Focus on Jesus. He loves you. There is far too much expectations on men; and this results in impatience, bitterness and hatred. I love to teach you what my Son has asked me. I bless you, my little ones, and thank you for responding to my call.

Notes & Reflections:

NOVEMBER 18, 1993
MESSAGE FROM OUR LORD

My dear ones, I come this night to tell you again of the love of My Father. This is the time of a great visitation during which many graces are bestowed upon you if you listen and respond. My dear ones, you do know the way to peace. It is simply to follow the commandments of My Father and your Father; to follow what I have asked of you and what I have given you through the example of My life. Take courage. Accept the strength which I give you through My spirit. Know that I am with you; that My mother walks with you, that Our holy angels surround you to protect you. Know that I speak the truth to you. As you follow this way of peace, you will be, and already are, light to the world. Again, I say take courage and continue, persevere and follow in My command. I bless you this night with the grace that you most need. I give you My mercy and My healing.

Notes & Reflections:

DECEMBER 2, 1993
MESSAGE FROM LADY

My dear little children, praise be Jesus. My little ones, do you realize that because of the current condition of the world, if I were to come to you only *one time* that no one would listen to my words of plea! But because my Son loves you so *unconditionally,* He has humbled Himself to allow Me to come to you in a very present way to help you and ask your *unconditional love.* As your mother, I ask you to humble yourself to my Son. Go before Him in the Blessed Sacrament, smother Him with love in order that He will mitigate what is to come. Do not ask Him to fulfill your personal needs. He knows what you need for eternal happiness. Simply love Him and praise Him for He is your God. He is the Son of God. You have all become too indifferent, failing to realize who is your God. Your mortal human ways have caused division and scattered destructiveness because of your own desire to control.

I am now pleading with you in these last days that I am permitted to be here, to love Jesus and follow His ways outlined in Scripture. Is there not one of you who will love my Son without expecting consolation in return? How can I help you if when He tests you, you will not allow me to be your mediatrix of grace? Put aside your human desires and look to that which is divine.

I bless you, my little ones. I love you, and I am thanking you for taking seriously this call to love. Peace to you in the name of Jesus! He is your God whether you wish to acknowledge that or not. The day will come that all will know the truth. Peace.

Notes & Reflections:

DECEMBER 2, 1993
MESSAGE FROM OUR LORD

My dear ones, I want you to know again this night I am with you always. When you cannot see Me, when you cannot feel Me and even when you cannot hear Me, I am with you. I thank you for your persevering prayer. I thank you for your love of My Father, of Me, of Our

Holy Spirit, and of My mother. I bless you, My dear ones, this night with My merciful peace and with My joy that is beyond your understanding. Know that I am with you.
Notes & Reflections:

DECEMBER 9, 1993
MESSAGE FROM OUR LADY

My dear children, I am your Mother of the Immaculate Conception. I am your Mother of Joy. Praise be Jesus! Praise His holy name. My little ones, you are all called to a life of purity; a life free of sin; a life filled with joy, happiness and peace. Satan would like you to dwell on your sins. He would like you to live in shame, guilt and be unforgiving to yourselves and others. In prayer you will realize that Jesus loves you and is calling you not to sin, shame or guilt, but to freedom, joy, purity and forgiveness.

Receive His love. Utilize the sacrament of reconciliation and you will be like new born babes. Seek to be pure, my little ones. Pray, live in His faith and love one another unconditionally. Jesus will grace you with purity if you desire this virtue. I bless you, my little ones, and ask you to pray for purity so you will be free from the stain of sin and be whole and happy. Thank you, my little ones, for responding to my call, a call to purity. Peace.
Notes & Reflections:

DECEMBER 16, 1993
MESSAGE FROM OUR LADY

My dear little children, praise be Jesus! My little ones, please be calm. Rest in my Son's sacred heart. If you lift your head from His yoke, you will be wounded. Focus on Him! Jesus is your protection, love and intimate friend. Blessed are those who are meek and mild of heart, simple, yet so consumed by the flame of His sacred heart. You are all called to be blest by being meek and humble of heart. Focus on my Son. He will temper your vices with love. Love will filter into your soul and consume your entire being.

My little ones, know I take your petitions to my Son. I will always take your petitions and present you as a loving mother would. You will never be forgotten by Jesus. Even if all forget you, Jesus will never forget you. You are precious in His eyes and He desires you so tremendously. Tonight I bless you with the grace of meekness. Thank you my little ones. I bless you in the name of my Son, who has allowed me to be here for you. Thank you for responding to this call to meekness and humbleness of heart. Peace.
Notes & Reflections:

DECEMBER 16, 1993
MESSAGE FROM OUR LORD

My dear ones, this night I come to encourage you to continue on your journey. You know I am with you every step of the way. I have said this to you so often. I encourage you now to believe what I say, to continue in courage this journey of yours. My dear ones, I so often see, though, there is so little joy within you. Yours is the best of all joy. You are God's children. You are redeemed by My blood. This is the cause of your joy. This is the reality of joy; and yet so often I see so little joy within you. And so this night I say to you: "Be joyful children of God." Know that you are not alone. Know that you are strengthened through Our Holy Spirit. Know that I continue to send to you My mother who prays for you daily. I bless you, My dear ones, with My peace. I again share with you the joy of God.

Notes & Reflections:

DECEMBER 23, 1993
MESSAGE FROM OUR LADY

My dear children, be at peace. Be at peace. For it is the peace of my Son that I bring to you this night. As you receive Him this night, you receive the Prince of Peace, who is born upon the altars of the world every day so that He can be born within your hearts and souls everyday. I ask you to prepare for Him everyday. Receive Him everyday in His Eucharistic presence. My Jesus, the King of Kings, comes to you each day in this humblest of forms. Can you not prepare each day to receive Him with the same fervor you prepare for His birth? My little ones, my Jesus comes to you each day to fill you with His peace, His love, His joy. Come and adore Him within the tabernacle of your hearts and souls. I invite you to come each day to the King of all Kings, my Jesus, and allow Him Who is peace to dwell within you, filling you with His Joy and His love. I love you, my sweet children, I love you. Prepare to receive our King. Thank you for having so lovingly responded to my call.

Notes & Reflections:

DECEMBER 30, 1993
MESSAGE FROM OUR LADY

My dear little children, praise be Jesus. My little ones, how blest are you to know Jesus. How blest you are that He in His infinite mercy and countenance graces you with His divine love. My little children, Jesus IS YOUR SAVIOUR. Do you not see interiorly how free you are because of the newborn babe. Remember always, my little children, that through Him you can serve this world; all His children in need. But without my Son, you cannot serve the world with love, even though humanly you can serve. Only through Jesus can you love. And only through His love can you truly serve those in need in this world.

I love you, my little children, and I give to you my greatest treasure, my Son, my heart. Take this precious gift, and cultivate the love He has given to you through loving one another. Thank you, my little children, for your prayers. Use this time of grace wisely by always examining your actions. Always they should be actions of love for others, yourself and most importantly, my Son. Love Him first above yourself and yourself for Him. Then you can love others, and your actions will be fruitful in His love. I bless you in the name of Emmanuel, your God Who is with you! Thank you for your response to my call. Peace.

Notes & Reflections:

DECEMBER 30, 1993
MESSAGE FROM OUR LORD

My dear ones, I come this night to encourage you to live now in My Kingdom. Abandon the trappings of this world. Live My Kingdom now! My dear ones, there is no need for you to wait. Live now in My Kingdom. Be truly children of God whom you are. Live My peace and My joy. Live My compassion and My mercy. Live daily the love that Our Holy Spirit places within you. Look at each other through My eyes. Look beyond the trappings and see the reality of your life with God. Allow this to be the goal for your new year. As you live more in My Kingdom now, you will truly be in My Kingdom... My Kingdom, through you, can begin when you say yes by the way you live. I bless you at the end of this your year. I give you My strength, and My mercy, and My perseverance as you begin your new year.
Notes & Reflections:

JANUARY 13, 1994
MESSAGE FROM OUR LADY

My dear little children, praise be Jesus! My little, little children, know how precious the gift of family is given from my Son. Always unite in harmony and love your family members. Each person in your family is a special gift to you from God. Each is special in God's love and very important in His eyes. Always unite with each other in your family. It is an important key to salvation. Where there is love there is God. Look beyond your differences and know how God created each one of you in love. See His love in your family and share this love with others in your community. I bless you, my little ones, in the name of my Son, and I pray for your strength to persevere in God's love. Love saves; love heals and love conquers. Love is victory. Love your family. Love God, and thank Him for the many blessings He has bestowed upon you through the family. Peace. Thank you for responding to my call.
Notes & Reflections:

JANUARY 20, 1994
MESSAGE FROM OUR LADY

My dear little children, praise be Jesus! My little ones, Jesus is your treasure. Adore Him with all of your hearts. Rest in Him allowing Him to whisper words of love and courage while you adore Him in the most Blessed Sacrament. How my Son has been waiting for you in the tabernacles of the world. He loves you so much. You are very important to Him. Tend to Him and rest in Him.

My little ones, as this grace period soon will end, it is very important to focus on Jesus, love one another as a family and support each other with ways of love. If you lose your focus from distraction, you will become confused. I ask you to concentrate on your intimate relationship with my Son, and do not deviate from your love for Him. He will protect you and He will be with you. Focus on Jesus as these unusual events unfold. Pray, pray, pray to not be tested; and that you will never lose sight of my Son. Pray for peace, unity, harmony, purity and honesty. I bless you, my little ones, in the name of Jesus. Thank you for responding to my call.

Notes & Reflections:

JANUARY 27, 1994
MESSAGE FROM OUR LADY

My dear little children, praise be Jesus! My little ones, I come to you in joy but also in sadness. Joy because God exists and He loves you. You do not fully comprehend the depth of His love, but He does love you, each one of you. But I come to you in sadness, because I have been allowed to come here to plead with you that your hearts would change. I have asked that you seek intimacy with my Son and to make evident changes in your life that were not ways of love and harmony. I have tried to teach you and guide you in the ways of my Son, pleading that you would not seek ways of power and worldly goals but that which is Divine. Many continue to take lightly my requests. I wish with all my love to help you but you, through your free will, must desire this heavenly way. Please, my little ones, my Son has not allowed me to come for little purpose. Please take seriously my words.

Your eternal life depends on your heart's desire. Where is Jesus in your life? Is He first? Pray to whose who rest in peace, for they know the depth of my Son's love which you have not yet grasped. Pray they intercede for you, that you may love as my Son. Remember, my little ones, Jesus is mercy; but if you will not accept His mercy, He will have no choice than to be a God of justice.

I bless you and love you, my little ones. Please do not ignore my plea for love and interior change through God's grace. Your life and your safety depends on securing eternal bliss. Thank you for responding to my call.

(*who rest in peace - meaning those souls having entered into Heaven.)

Notes & Reflections:

JANUARY 27, 1994
MESSAGE FROM OUR LORD

My dear ones, I ask you this night to again listen to Me speaking to you; not only in this way here in this place, but in My sacred scriptures, in My Most Blessed Sacrament and within your heart. In the innermost urgings of your heart it is I; know that. Be assured of that. I do not leave you orphan. I give you My faith and Our Holy Spirit, and I, Myself, am with you. Even in the dark times I am there. Step out in faith as you listen to Me. Do not be timid, but brave. I am with you, but My dear ones, if you do not listen to Me you will listen to other voices which will lead you from Me. Listen and you will hear. Trust and you will understand. This night I bless you again with My mercy, and give you the courage to continue in perseverance in your journey.

Notes & Reflections:

FEBRUARY 3, 1994
MESSAGE FROM OUR LADY

My dear little children, praise be Jesus! My little ones, I bring you good news. Jesus' love is everlasting and you can rest totally in Him. Thanks be to God for His kindness and mercy which are everlasting. I hear your plea, my dear ones. Know that even though there are many of you who struggle, there is hope in my Son. Do not be discouraged. The good news is that you belong to God. When you hope and trust in my Son, you can rest in peace with confidence that love and mercy are yours for all eternity. Inner conflict and struggles may unveil; but know God loves you and wishes for you to rise to a level of wholeness. Evil will be weeded out from the good. You are all called to be pure and whole; to love.

There are many kinds of love but I speak of a love of charity. This love is kept for love of God and is supreme and sovereign. You may not fully comprehend His love, but I ask you to rejoice in His love for you because His love and mercy endures. I present you this night to my Son with love and as your mother. I ask you to focus on Him. Love Him with all your hearts and rejoice that His mercy endures forever. Peace my little ones. Thank you. Know Our peace, love and support will always sustain you. Thank you, little ones, for responding to my Son's call and mine. Peace!

Notes & Reflections:

FEBRUARY 3, 1994
MESSAGE FROM OUR LORD

My dear ones, I ask you this night to listen to Me. My dear ones, because of the gift My Father has given, I have overcome the world. I ask you again to listen. I have overcome, through the gracious mercy of My Father, all that you are struggling with, even your sin. Listen, My dear ones, I give you My mercy. I give you My love. I give you My consolation. My dear ones, please accept these gifts. Do not be consumed with your sin; with your anxiety. Come to Me; come to your understanding Lord; come to the One Who has died for you; come to the One Who is raised to new life for you. Accept My love for you; accept the gift of redemption within My love and you will be in the light of the Son of God, and you will reflect the love and the joy, and the hope, and the peace that My Father offers you.

My dear ones, I AM WITH YOU NOW AND ALWAYS! Listen! Listen! I bless you again this night for your journey. Trust in Me. I will never disappoint you. I will give you all you need!

Notes & Reflections:

FEBRUARY 10, 1994
MESSAGE FROM OUR LADY

My dear little children, praise be Jesus! My words to you are direct and simple this night. I come before you asking you to pray that the challenges my Son presents to you for your good be fulfilled through abandonment. Please, my little ones, seek to surrender every day and accept God's love. Pray!! Do not be distracted with your personal issues. God knows what you need. Surrender all to Him. Pray that you will surrender and that His challenges of love will be fulfilled through your acceptance and abandonment. Please do not be deceived these days, my little ones. Satan would like you to be deceived. I speak the truth, and you will know this truth through prayer and surrendering to divine providence. I love you my little children. God loves you. I bless you in the name of Him Who sent me. Please pray that you will surrender unto God and accept His divine will designed especially for your happiness. Thank you for responding to my call. Peace.

Notes & Reflections:

FEBRUARY 17, 1994
MESSAGE FROM OUR LADY

My dear little children, praise be Jesus! My little ones, during this Lenten season know that the Lord loves you. This season is one of love. Give to Him your hearts in love. It is to be a Lenten season of giving, forgiving, love and mortification. Do not be blinded by that which my Son calls for you to live. Pray for the virtues to live as He, virtues of patience, humility, love, charity and self-mortification and meekness. My Jesus is your Saviour. Pray that you will see Him as He is. I bless you, my little children, and take your petitions to my Son's Sacred Heart. I pray they will be fulfilled during this Lenten season of love.

Most importantly, my prayer for you is to look beyond to that which is Divine, for your glory in Jesus through love and mortification, a special charitable love which will never fail you but will always sustain you. Thank you for responding to my call. Peace. Ad deum.

Notes & Reflections:

FEBRUARY 17, 1994
MESSAGE FROM OUR LORD

My dear ones, I come to you this night to encourage you to choose life, the life which My Father and Our Holy Spirit give to you. This life, My dear ones, can only truly be lived if you die to your selfishness. This life to be fully lived needs to come from embracing your cross. To the world, this is folly. To the world, this is meaningless but, My dear ones, the world does not know what true life is. This night I strengthen you so that you may carry the cross of your daily lives and so that you may embrace it. I have given you the example, and I have shown you where the cross leads. It leads to eternal life, life to its fullest measure. There is nothing to fear. Even your weakness and unwillingness can be overcome, if you give those to Me. I love you and I encourage you during this time to choose life by embracing your cross. You are not alone. I am carrying it with you. I bless each of you this night with My mercy and My love. Be at peace, My dear ones, be at peace!

Notes & Reflections:

FEBRUARY 24, 1994
MESSAGE FROM OUR LADY
TO THE WORLD

My dear little children, praise be Jesus! I am your Mother of Joy who so desires you to live in a world of peace. But peace does not exist because there is division. There is division because of the conflict which exists on the moral values in the world.

My little, little children, do not alter your standards of following the gospel in order to satisfy the needs of others. Never deviate from the truth of His word. You cannot please men by jeopardizing your freedom and living deceitful ways of life. The only way to freedom is by living the truth outlined by my Son. He has given you His word. You cannot change His words and live dishonest lives and conceive that peace could even exist.

There is only ONE way and that way is the way of my Son in His word of the gospel. He is your God. There is only one God. I plead with you that you hold fast to His word and not to deviate from His stance on truth or you will suffer tremendously through the hands of man. I love you, my little ones, and bless you. I desire you to be happy and free, but you must return to God and live the truth of His word. Killings of all sorts*, greed, abuse, selfishness, anger, malice, dishonesty, adultery and other sexual disgraces self-induced and those of children, men and women* are vices which prevent your freedom. Reconcile your sins and live in His truth. Thank you for responding to my call. Ad Deum.

*Our Lady wanted it to be known that the above 'Killings of all sorts' included abortions; and sexual disgraces of 'men and women' were those of homosexuality.
Notes & Reflections:

MARCH 3, 1994
MESSAGE FROM OUR LADY

My dear little children, praise be Jesus! My little ones, know you are children of God. Seek to follow the ways of Christian perfection, and walk away from the ways of wickedness. God loves you. Trust in God and follow His way. The challenges and enticements of life result in shortcomings without the love and hope in God. Do not turn your heart away from God. Hope in Him. During these times where God is unveiling His mercy, you need to be strong in the gift of His faith and be secure in His hope. You must not sway in your decision to be a child of God, nor be ashamed to follow His truth when confronted with controversial topics of moral values. You must hope and trust in God. You must speak the truth of His word. It is your only security. If you seek to please man while avoiding the truth of God outlined in His word of the gospel, then you will jeopardize your freedom and position of attaining eternal bliss at the time of your final judgment before Him. I bless you, my little ones, in the name of Jesus. Thank you for responding to my call.
Notes & Reflections:

MARCH 3, 1994
MESSAGE FROM OUR LORD

My dear ones, I am with you again this night to remind you that I come under the title of Jesus of Mercy, not justice. I wish to give you My mercy. My dear ones, I ask you to accept the gift of My mercy in your life, for none of you could withstand the justice of My Father. NOW is the time of mercy. I encourage you - respond to this gift. Come to Me with all of who you are and I will heal you, and forgive you, and comfort you. My mercy is for you and for all who allow this gift to be in their hearts. My Father is not stingy with this gift He gives to you through Me. In turn, My dear ones, I encourage you to be generous in your mercy toward others. You block My mercy when you are unmerciful. Look again at each other and see the dear child of God which each of you is. I bless you this night with My peace. I take from you this night your fear. I love you with My mercy this night.
Notes & Reflections:

MARCH 10, 1994
MESSAGE FROM OUR LADY

My dear little children, praise be Jesus! Thank you, my little ones, for inviting me to be with you. Thanks be to God who has allowed me to come in His name. Tonight, my little ones, I have two requests: Firstly, I ask you to unite with me in prayer for my beloved priests who are loyal to my Son and who suffer tremendously. Their pain is endless because of their loyalty. Pray for them especially during these times of uncertainty and troubles. I love my priests. Join me please in prayer. Secondly, my little children, I must tell you not to trust in deceitful words. If you focus on Jesus, trust in Him, abandon yourself unto Him and practice His words of truth, you will not be deceived but live healthy, joyful lives. Change is needed, not only in words, but in action. Give unconditionally, simply and lovingly to others without seeking reward or consolation for your efforts. Wickedness must be replaced with ways of holiness. If change is not accomplished, then the time will come that your sorrow will result at the hands of wicked disposition which will be its blame. I bless you, my little ones. I love you and take your petitions to my Son. Thank you for your prayers for peace, and thank you for responding to my call. Peace. Ad deum.
Notes & Reflections:

MARCH 10, 1994
MESSAGE FROM OUR LORD

My dear ones, I come to you this night to make again a request. Stay close to Me! Come near Me! You need My protection more than you know. Try not to stray and be diluted and disheartened by transitory happiness. My dear ones, the further you are from Me, the weaker you become and the more a prey you are to the evil one. Stay close to Me. I am your strength. My Father has given Me to you, and I have laid down My life for you. Stay close! Allow Me to be your strength and your protection. I love you, and it saddens Me when you hurt yourself by allowing the temptations to overcome you. My dear, dear ones, please do not think that you can walk this journey alone. Do not think that you can take on the evil one by yourself. Stay close to Me and then the fear will leave you and be replaced by My peace. This peace I give you this night along with My healing mercy. I AM WITH YOU ALWAYS! BE WITH ME ALWAYS!

Notes & Reflections:

MARCH 17, 1994
MESSAGE FROM OUR LADY

My dear children, praise be Jesus! My little ones, you continue to pray that the will of God be done in your lives. Doing the will of God involves the following: If you are religious, then being obedient to your superiors is doing the will of the Father. If you are a superior, pray for discernment and use prudence and love. If you are married, then be obedient to each other as spouses in the sacrament of marriage, and teach your children to love and follow the way of truth outlined in my Son's word in the gospel. If you are single, live pure, holy lives consecrated to God. Be honest and treat others with dignity. Help the poor and elderly and the young. And if you have been blessed with resources of wealth, intellect, management skills and graces to help His needy, then unite together and give to His less fortunate. They suffer as representation of the humiliated Jesus.

Protect my unborn through love and unity. Teach my youth and unite all your resources in harmony. Help my Son in His mission of mercy. It is the way to peace. Peace cannot exist if there is no change in moral values and in unity. I continue to plead to God for His mercy and love. There is no time like the present to commence these activities. Prayer and love will restrain His hand of punishment from the lack of love. It is the only way. He is your God, the same God of Abraham, Isaac and Jacob. If you implore His mercy and love, all can be mitigated; for everything is contingent on prayer. Thank you for responding to my call. Peace. Ad deum.

Notes & Reflections:

MARCH 17, 1994
MESSAGE FROM OUR LORD

My dear ones, I am here with you this night to encourage you to live in faith the words that I speak to you, the words that are truly of My Father, the words that will resonate within your very heart. Live these words, live this faith and be the example and the light to those I send into your life. My dear ones, faith is not knowledge. Faith is believing the word of someone else. Believe the words that I speak. They will give you eternal life; they will give you peace; they will give you My strength. Come to Me, and I will refresh you. Come to Me. I will heal you. Come to Me and receive the forgiveness that is yours. My dear ones, do not wander aimlessly away from Me. Keep close to Me. I will give you life. I bless you this night with the peace of My Father and of Our Holy Spirit. Take courage, my dear ones, take courage!

Notes & Reflections:

MARCH 24, 1994
MESSAGE FROM OUR LADY

My dear little children, praise be Jesus! I am your Mother of Joy who brings you the joy of my Son, your Jesus, your Saviour. My little ones, you are seeking God but He is everywhere. Everything speaks of Him to you. Everything offers Him to you. He surrounds you. He walks with you and He is within you. He is your living God. He lives with you and yet you are trying to seek Him. This is because you are seeking your own idea of God, even though you have Him in reality. My dear little children, love God as He is. You are straining after vain imaginations of who God is and are not allowing Him to dwell with you. Do you not see that all you do, all you suffer and all you envelop daily, are the mysteries under which God gives Himself to you? Put aside your falsehoods and the sweet enticements of the world, and live in His Truth. Accept daily His living presence of love through all you encounter, and in all you do, and in everything that surrounds you. His divine perfection of design is for you. Live it fully to the best of your ability in His love. Do not miss the moment because of false imaginations. I thank His blessed name for allowing me to be with you. It is because of His love and divine mercy. Thank you for responding to my call. Ad deum.

Notes & Reflections:

APRIL 7, 1994
MESSAGE FROM OUR LADY

My dear little children, praise be Jesus! I would like all of you to know that living God's love may seem to be a mystery but will not remove you from the gift of your humanness. The mystery of His love allows you the freedom to be the human being He created. God loves you as you are. Please first recognize His love for you in your humanness. That is how you are brought to fulfillment and union in the Triune God. Please be who you are and live in God's love. Live life in God, for God and love one another in God and for God.

Keep in mind my words to you on moral values, deception and purity. Peace cannot exist as long as killings of all sorts continue and ways of demoralization occur. You are all called to live a perfection of love through purity, fidelity and wholeness. Please heed my words of truth; for there will be no choice other than to live a time of great difficulty. This difficult time is extremely close to being unveiled and will be a result of my Son's mercy. Begin gathering necessary resources now to sustain you in living the way of love. I wish for all my children to have a time of preparation and opportunity to choose life through His love. Peace and love little children. Thank you for responding to my call. Ad deum.

Notes & Reflections:

APRIL 14, 1994
MESSAGE FROM OUR LADY

My dear little children, praise be Jesus! My little ones, so many of my children are scattering instead of joining together in prayer. The commitment to prayer I have invited you to is life-long. It cannot be temporary or only in the time of need. Do you not see that through the gift of prayer you are able to express the many virtues my Son graces you? Prayer is simple; but I cannot help you unless you take on the commitment, as I have invited you several times. It is a daily commitment of time to be with my Son, desiring change and challenge. It is listening in openness... my Son speaks to all, even in silence.

My little, little children, realize how patient my Son is with you. Please, how many warnings have I presented throughout the ages that have been softened or even mitigated because of prayer, response and my Son's patience? Take seriously my call to prayer, unity and change. Perhaps you have become too comfortable with my presence. Please recognize the gift He has given to you by allowing me to be here and please respond. It is because of my Son's mercy and love for you. Do not neglect Him or take lightly His requests; for the time will arrive quickly when you will wish to hear my words and will no longer. My Son loves you. Please do not become lax in prayer. Please live His words to the best of your ability. Please, please, please pray with all your heart. Peace. Thank you for responding to my call. Ad deum.

Notes & Reflections:

APRIL 14, 1994
MESSAGE FROM OUR LORD

My dear ones, know that I come in love this night to you. As you celebrate My resurrection in your heart, I encourage you to listen to the truth. Listen to Our Holy Spirit speaking to your heart. Listen to My living word in the scripture and be permeated with the truth of Myself in the Eucharist. The truth, My dear ones, will sometimes be very difficult for you to listen to for it will require of you change; it will require of you abandonment. It will require of you true humility. Know that I speak the truth of My Father to all and this truth touches each person's heart, but it is up to each one to respond or not. I ask you this night to listen to the truth and to respond. There are many who disguise their lives with half truths. My dear ones, you need not be afraid of these people. I encourage you simply to come before Me in My Most Blessed Sacrament There you will know what is true and what is false. Know that your Risen Lord - know that I am with you in a very special way during these days. Take advantage of this time, My dear ones. I bless you this night with My peace and My mercy. Know that I take you, each of you, to My heart in love.

Notes & Reflections:

APRIL 21, 1994
MESSAGE FROM OUR LADY

My dear little children, praise be Jesus! My little ones, please surrender to my Son. If you would surrender unto His mercy in your misery, you would see His wondrous works unveil. My words are simple; and I wish to help you be happy and free, but you need to surrender and trust God. If you are miserable, then the opportunity to surrender to my Son's mercy exists at this present moment. Do not delay. The wonders of God will unfold before you and you all can live in the glory of God in harmony. But if you do not lay your miseries at the foot of the cross, embracing who you are and your need for His mercy, you will continue to live in a world of division and destruction.

Call on Jesus. Call on His mercy. Surrender to His mercy. Trust in Him and see the wonders of God unfold. There is no time such as the present to accept God's mercy. Please, children, accept God's merciful love through surrendering and trusting in Him. Thank you for responding to my call.

Notes & Reflections:

APRIL 21, 1994
MESSAGE FROM OUR LORD

My dear ones, I am here again tonight with you to encourage you to continue in your journey. Know that I am with you, that I, Myself, through My Eucharist, am your food for the journey. Know with all of your hearts that it is truly I, your Lord, in the Eucharist, truly present with you, and to you, and for you always. I am with you always; and in this gift of Myself to you I show My love and My constancy. I invite you ever closer to Me in My Eucharist. Feed upon Me, become one with Me, and I will truly give you rest, and peace, and joy. In My Eucharist, I am your strength. I bless you this night, each of you, with My mercy and My love.

Notes & Reflections:

APRIL 28, 1994
MESSAGE FROM OUR LADY

My dear little children, praised be Jesus! My little ones, you are so consumed with the fear of my authenticity that you are failing to see how the Lord in His humility has allowed me to be here with you. Focus on Jesus in the Eucharist and trust in Him. Fear God, that you might offend Him in self-pride and self-righteousness. Be humble. Love Him. Implore His mercy. Adore Him in the most Blessed Sacrament. But do not fear whether you are being deceived in trying to authenticate my presence. I belong to God. You belong to God. Remember a house not of God will divide itself. Put your fears to rest and hope in the resurrected Christ! There is no time for fear. There is time for change. You are all novices in the knowledge of His most merciful love. Remove yourself and allow my Son to be your God. Remove the idolatry you have formed of yourself and placed higher than He. He is your God. And I have been allowed to come here to implore you to focus on Him, trust Him and return back to Him.

I plead with you not to advocate abortion as a form of population control. My little ones, please notice the destruction, and desolation and desecration which results from destroying the temple of God. Life is your gift. Life is a treasure and not a burden. Abuse it, and my Son will take it away from you. Please heed my warning in His name. Please pray before

my Son in the most Blessed Sacrament, and implore His mercy and grace to enlighten you with His truth of life. Peace, my little ones, and thank you for responding to this most serious call. Ad deum.
Notes & Reflections:

APRIL 28, 1994
MESSAGE FROM OUR LORD

My dear ones, I come to you this night to warn you against pride. Pride wars against My very presence within you. My dear ones, I encourage you this night to follow the example that I have set for you, that My mother has set for you. Beware of spiritual pride. Know with all of your hearts, My dear ones, that without the love of My Father you could do nothing. My dear ones, in humility and honesty before God you will please Him. In humility you will honor Him. Through humility will you attract others to Him. My dear ones, please know that I can truly walk with you only when you are humble. When you are full of pride you walk alone. Come to Me; learn from Me; listen to Me, and you will be pleasing to My Father. I bless you this night, My dear ones, with the grace to open your eyes and to see the ways in which you walk in pride. I give you also the strength to now walk humbly with your God.
Notes & Reflections:

MAY 5, 1994
MESSAGE FROM OUR LADY

My dear children, praise be Jesus! My little, little children, pray that God's mercy make you clean and turn you away from your sinful ways. You are little children acting as if you are all-knowing and powerful in God's love. Return to God in littleness and depend on Him to lead you. Pray before Him in the most Blessed Sacrament for truth of your deceitful ways, so that you will be able to repent in humility and be made whole. My Son loves you and I wish to help you and save you from walking towards a life of human destruction. Allow me to bring you to my Son. Allow me to present your beauty of a child. In order to do this, you must humbly submit to changing your deceitful ways of power, reputation, acceptance of man, success for your glory to that which belongs to God. Return to God and at all costs seek to be obedient to Him. Only those who risk even the chance of hardship for God, in obedience to following the truth of His word, are true commanders in His army of love. It is time you put into action your love for Him. You must be willing to give everything up for God to be true imitators of Christ. Peace little ones, peace!
Notes & Reflections:

MAY 12, 1994
MESSAGE FROM OUR LADY

My dear little children, praise be Jesus! My little ones, pray with all your heart during these next nine days that you be enlightened by the gifts of the Holy Spirit. Pray always for God's gift of gratitude. It is in gratitude to Him that you shall receive more gifts. Always be thankful for God's goodness and love. My Son loves you tremendously. He has not forsaken you. Be whole in Him. Be little children. To be little is to simply "be" and love God, trusting in Him. Be totally dependent on Him as a child. You utilize your intellect far more than your heart. Pray with your heart, process everything through your heart. You are relying on your mind instead of your heart, especially in reflection, which causes resistance and lack of joy. God's grace is made abundant to you. His way is simple. It is time you pray for fortitude and surrender to God's will at all times. Procure your relationship now with God as a dependent child, in littleness and in gratitude. Thank you, little ones, for responding to my call. My blessings. Peace.

Notes & Reflections:

MAY 12, 1994
MESSAGE FROM OUR LORD

My dear ones, I come to you on this day in which you celebrate My ascension, to assure you to be joyful, for I am coming to you again. It is I, your Lord, Who is coming to you. My dear ones, you do not have to wait, however, until I come at the end of your world; for I come to you daily, if you allow it. I walk every minute with you. I am with you in My Eucharist. I am with you in My word. I am with you in My Most Blessed Sacrament.

My dear ones, I am always coming to you. Never forget My presence with you, and as I did with My disciples of old, I do with you this night, My disciples of now -- I send you into your world to be My instruments of peace, of mercy, of love, of joy, of truth, of compassion, and above all, at this time, be My disciples of hope. Preach these gifts not by your words but with your life. Know that I give you My strength and that I am coming to you each moment, if you allow Me to. Open your hearts and receive Me. I give you My peace, dear ones, and the grace of perseverance. I love you!

Notes & Reflections:

MAY 19, 1994
MESSAGE FROM OUR LADY

My dear little children, praise be Jesus! My Son who has given everything to the Father for love of you, even His life, asks that you give everything to Him, for love of Him. What, little children, are you willing to risk for love of God? Many of my children currently say they are willing to risk all for God, but at this present time only a small percentage of the world's population are truly willing. Are you one who will soon turn away from my Son and deny Him?

My little children, there is no time left. You are no longer listening to my words and it is almost too late. The brilliance of the moon has begun to reflect that of bloodshed. I urge you to pray like you have never prayed before. Pray and ask the Holy Spirit for counsel, understanding, fear of God, fortitude, piety, wisdom and knowledge of His truth. I want to help you, little ones. I love you. You must change right now and live in God's peace or it will be too late. Do not fear but LISTEN to my words and unite in the family, pray and love. Simplify your lives and live for God who loves you. Bless you, little ones. I remain with you. Peace.

Notes & Reflections:

MAY 26, 1994
MESSAGE FROM OUR LADY

My dear little children, praise be Jesus! My little ones, if you had knowledge of salvation you would be freed from fear and from your enemies. The Holy Spirit, through His gift of charity, gives you understanding and knowledge. He enlightens you to rejoice in God. He sanctifies you. Those who live in the Holy Spirit live in gratitude for graces received. I desire to help you and to intercede for you, but you must LISTEN to my words and respond to my call. Currently the vast majority of my children whom I desire to help are hearing only what they choose to hear.

Please listen to ALL my words of truth. You cannot only recognize my plea but must respond through acceptance of my words and living them. I tell you again, little ones, you must be willing to risk all for love of God. My Son freed you by giving all to God for love of you. He has given everything to you. He has provided for you. But now you are not willing to give back to God what He has given to you because you are slaves to fear and do not trust my Son. How can I help you, if you select the words I speak which you choose to hear? Listen little children. Listen to my motherly call and respond. Do not be afraid to give yourself totally to God. He will always provide for you and fill you with joy. Do not be slaves to fear and materialism. If you give yourself unconditionally to my Son, you will allow me to be a mother who will provide the best for her children. Peace little ones. Thank you for responding to my call.

Notes & Reflections:

MAY 26, 1994
MESSAGE FROM OUR LORD

My dear ones, as I come to you this night through the grace of God Our Father, I extend My mercy to you. I invite you now in the quiet of your heart to answer this question, a question that I asked the blind beggar long ago. As I ask this question of you and as you answer in your heart, I assure you I am listening as I listened to him, and so I ask each of you, 'What do you wish Me to do for you?' (A long pause followed). As I said to him so long ago I say to each of you this night - you may leave this place in My peace, your faith is making you whole. My mercy, My dear ones, is the gift that I give to you. It is through My mercy and through your being merciful to others that you will be healed from that which is keeping you from Me. Know that I am with you, that I wish you to be whole, and that I love you. Live in My peace!

Notes & Reflections:

JUNE 2, 1994
MESSAGE FROM LADY

My dear little children, praise be Jesus who loves you! Praise be to the Father who loves you! Praise be to the Holy Spirit who loves and feeds your soul! My little ones, you must dive into my most Immaculate Heart *immediately!* I wish for you all to be consecrated to my Immaculate Heart and to be safe and free! Please little ones. I can no longer hold back the hand of my Son from the sorrow incurred on His Sacred Heart. Little, little children, you are not listening to my words. You are not living my messages. Do you not see how I desire to help you? There are few who trust in God. There are few living in His faith. Please, little children, I urgently ask you to heed my call. Adore Jesus in the most Blessed Sacrament. Pray to the Father and trust in His most tender love. I love you, little ones, and I have given you many messages to assist you in knowing His truth. Live the messages and pray you will not be tested, but free and happy. I bless you, little children, and thank you for responding to my call.

Notes & Reflections:

JUNE 9, 1994
MESSAGE FROM OUR LADY

My dear little children, praise be Jesus! My little ones, if you only hear the word of God, you are not justified in His sight. Only those who observe and live His word will be justified. You will not be justified through your works, but on the basis of your faith. It is your faith and trust in God which will make you righteous. You need to live the messages of God. Live His word. You cannot only hear it. You cannot wear an external image of holiness. God sees all things. It is the spirit of your works and your living faith in God which will make you holy. My little ones, all your hidden works will be judged. You cannot hide from God. All good and evil will be weeded out, and everyone will be revealed the truth of their incentives and state of faith. Graces flow out from my hands, dear children, desiring to help you. I love you. My Son loves you. He is loving and merciful. Children, lastly I ask you to pray for and support all my beloved priests. The sword is soon to pierce their hearts. Pray for your priests, bishops and cardinals. Pray for unity and peaceful resolutions between priests, bishops and cardinals. I bless you all, little children. Know God loves you. I have pointed the way to my Son. It is now your choice. Peace and thank you for responding to my call.

Notes & Reflections:

JUNE 9, 1994
MESSAGE FROM OUR LORD

My dear ones, I, your Lord, come to you this night to invite you to seek the holiness that My Father and Our Spirit and I wish to give you. Our holiness that We wish to give is unlike the holiness of the world. It is even unlike the holiness that you may be seeking. Do you not yet understand, My dear ones, that God's ways are not yours? Why do you continue to try to figure out what will happen? Trust, trust! Have I not died for you? Are you not precious in the sight of My Father? Have We not sent you Our Spirit? Why do you still insist on being anxious? This anxiousness blocks the holiness that We wish to give you. Listen to Me now. Allow this word to be your point of reflection in front of My most Blessed Sacrament. The word is this - SIMPLICITY! Come as a simple child and you will receive the holiness of God. I bless you this night; and I give you My courage to be simple, holy children of My Father.
Notes & Reflections:

JUNE 16, 1994
MESSAGE FROM OUR LADY

My dear little children, praise be Jesus! This time period designated by my Son is the last period in which I will be allowed to come to you, my little children, throughout the world. Please heed my words for I am a loving mother who desires to help you. Little, little children, pray! Pray! Pray! Pray for peace. Pray within your families. Unity, compassion and forgiveness are fruits from prayer in the family; and I have told you that you cannot have a pure heart unless you forgive. Be obedient to my beloved Pope and support my beloved priests. Serve my Son in joy and in freedom by contributing to the needs of others. Exercise hospitality. Rejoice in hope; endure in affliction; and persevere in prayer. Do not look for revenge in others but practice mercy. Mercy is the missing link to loving. My Son loves you, the Father loves you and desires you to recognize love. He is love. I take your petitions to the Sacred Heart of my Son and remind you to implore and invite the Holy Spirit to sanctify you. Thank you, little children, for your response to my call. I bless you in the name of my Son who has allowed me to be here. Peace. Ad deum.
Notes & Reflections:

JUNE 16, 1994
MESSAGE FROM OUR LORD

My dear ones, I am here with you again this night as your Lord and Saviour to plead with you. Listen to what I have asked, to what My mother continues to ask. Rededicate yourself, each of you, to prayer. You have become, My dear ones, so scattered. Come again before Me in My most Blessed Sacrament. Come to Me in that precious gift of Mine and My Father's, and Our Spirits to you. I see within your hearts and there is such a lack of forgiveness. My dear ones, look upon the crucifix. Remember what I have done for you. Imprint that picture within your mind. Press it to your heart and then see how terrible it is when you refuse to forgive yourself. I have died for you. Isn't that proof that you are forgiven? Come to Me through the sacrament of reconciliation and receive again My healing and My forgiveness. My dear ones, your lack of forgiveness of yourself blocks the mercy, and the joy, and the peace that I wish to give to you. Come to Me. Present yourself again to Me in My most Blessed Sacrament. I want with all of My heart to heal you, to strengthen you. With My strength you will forgive yourself, and so this night I bless you with the strength that you need, with the courage of My Holy Spirit. You again, this night, as you come to Me, can be a new creation. Be at peace now. Fear is useless.

Notes & Reflections:

JUNE 23, 1994
MESSAGE FROM OUR LADY

My dear little children, praise be Jesus! My little ones, please do not judge others. Be kind and loving. How you judge others reflects how you perceive yourself and would judge yourself. Focus on my Son. Please do not be distracted. If you are uncharitable you deny the love of Jesus and cannot wear the armor as a true follower of Him. To be in union with God you must pray, be charitable, be obedient and serve the needs of all through love. This requires faith and this union with God will never be destroyed. Little children, God loves you very much and desires that you know Him. Please be open to His love. Be eager to present yourself as acceptable to God. Please do not cause disgrace for others. Satan is desperately attempting to cause division. Anger, hatred, resentfulness, jealousy, malice and premeditated attempts to strip others of respect, dignity and self-esteem are the poisonous venoms to evil. Silence is the shield and love the sword to battle evil. I invite you to live ways of charity, patience, kindness and love towards one another. When you hurt others, you truly are hurting yourself. Peace little ones, and thank you for responding to my call. Ad deum.

Notes & Reflections:

JUNE 23, 1994
MESSAGE FROM OUR LORD

My dear ones, I am with you this night to again remind you that My mercy and the mercy of My Father and of Our Holy Spirit is with you, all of you, and each of you, always. You will not understand the bounds of My mercy. I ask you simply to accept this gift. As in the days of Zechariah, the mercy of God was so great that it seemed to him as impossible. Look what God's mercy can do! My dear ones, it is you who block the mercy of God. Allow God to be Who He is. Allow Me to truly be your Saviour and allow Our Holy Spirit to truly overwhelm you. You have no idea of what God's mercy can do. Please do not limit My mercy.

Notes & Reflections:

JUNE 30, 1994
MESSAGE FROM OUR LADY

My dear children, praise be Jesus! My little ones, humble yourself unto God. Those who humble themselves are exalted. My Son lifts the lowly to high places. Pray for humility like God. Surrender and trust in Him. Remember it is not your works that give God glory but your living faith and the spirit of your works. Use integrity to accomplish the works of God in His love. Integrity is honesty, sincerity and wholeness. Wholeness is abandoning yourself to live in union with God by doing His will. If you are humble in His sight, you will know His will, for you will know Him. Love is simple. Love is patience. Be patient with yourself as you surrender and grow in His love. God loves you, is tender, merciful and patient. He desires that the fruits of His love exemplify charity, joy and tranquility of peace in your life. Virtues and abundant graces will flow from His most Sacred Heart if you will allow them. My little children, allow God to be God. I am here to tell you God does exist and you are invited to His banquet through love and mercy. Please accept His invitation with a "yes" of loving. Peace and thank you for responding to my call. Ad deum.

Notes & Reflections:

JUNE 30, 1994
MESSAGE FROM OUR LORD

My dear ones, I, who have died for your sins, come this night to remind you that the healing that each of you needs the most is to be healed of your sin. My dear ones, sin is truly the cancer of the soul. Come to Me for healing of your sinfulness. Come, allow Me to forgive you. Know, My dear ones, that as you carry your sin you become more burdened, My joy cannot be within you, My peace is disrupted, and there is so much confusion and anxiety within. Please allow Me to forgive you. I am the Saviour of your soul. My prayer to My Father is that you stop sinning. Do not kill the life of Our Spirit within you with your sin. Receive and celebrate the great sacrament of reconciliation; and allow Me to forgive and to heal you. Know, My dear ones, that My spirit within you is more powerful than the spirit of evil which tempts you to sin. This night I give you the grace of My mercy to begin again and to walk in innocence and peace. I love you, and this night I take each of you to My heart.

Notes & Reflections:

JULY 7, 1994
MESSAGE FROM OUR LADY

My dear little children, praise be Jesus! My little ones, I desire all to be united to my Son. I desire all people to be happy and filled with joy and freedom. There are so many of my children who suffer because they have kept their distance from God. There are also many of my children who joyfully suffer in union with my Son as victims of His love. The cross is the connection to suffering with joy and love in union with my Son. Those who carry the cross of my Son are co-redemptors of His love through His salvation and mercy. Do not fear the cross. His cross is sweetness, charity, meekness, wisdom, justice, mercy and truth. Join together, little children, and unite with my Son in the joyful sufferings of love of your cross. Pray for all, my dear little ones, who have chosen to keep their distance from God. It is not God's desire they suffer the sufferings of a world without His love. The sufferings of love is one of joy, freedom, surrendering, abandonment even though painful many times. This is due to sanctification, purification, wholeness and becoming love.

Jesus is LOVE. He desires you to be Him - to be LOVE. Please do not fear the joy of His cross He desires to share with you. Pray, Pray, Pray. You will come to understand and love the cross in His love the closer you come to His light. Pray and you will desire His cross as He desires to gift you with it. It is not the cross of the suffering of the world but the suffering of LOVE. Thank you, little children, for responding to my call and peace be with you. Ad deum.

Notes & Reflections:

JULY 7, 1994
MESSAGE FROM OUR LORD

My dear ones, I come to you this night to remind you of the gift that My Father and Our Spirit has given to you through Me, your Saviour. It is the gift of mercy, My dear ones. This gift is not given to you for you to hold, but to be given through you to others. Truly, what you have been given, give as a gift. I encourage you to learn the depth of My mercy; the strength, the truth, the compassion, the joy of My mercy. Learn and live this gift. I bless you this night with My courage to accept My mercy, the mercy of your God, and then to live it and to give it to others. Peace, My dear ones. I am with you!

Notes & Reflections:

JULY 14, 1994
MESSAGE FROM OUR LADY

My dear little children, praise be Jesus! Thank you for coming to pray with reverence for God who awaits you in love and is the giver of all that is good. He is your creator. He is love. Little children, you also must love and have a mutual love for one another. You are the heirs to His inheritance. Be sincere and love one another with mutual affection. Look to do good, not evil. Be patient with each other's failings and live in harmony with one another. It is in God alone that you become victorious. That is why I invite you, little children, to turn to God, in child-like ways, to pray and to live in His merciful love, and to have a mutual affection towards one another. Please do not try the patience of others. You must all share in the gift of patience and self-denial to be sole heirs of God's righteousness.

My children, you know to pray. Do not delay. Take the initiative, in God's grace and pray, especially my little, little ones. Please pray, little children, everyday for your parents, family and for peace. The little children shall be instruments of salvation through prayer, the rosary and love. Do not rejoice over the failings of others but in meekness and in love show mercy.

Rejoice in what is good, not in what is evil. Pray! Blessings of God my little ones. Peace and thank you for responding to my call. Ad deum.
Notes & Reflections:

JULY 14, 1994
MESSAGE FROM OUR LORD

My dear ones, I come to you this night, your Lord and Saviour to speak to your heart, to say to you how often you take upon yourself yokes and burdens which are not the ones that I ask you to bear. My dear ones, you are scattered within yourselves. Come back to Me, listen to what I speak to your heart. This will give you comfort and peace, and then go and do what I ask. The anxiety you have is never from Me, but My dear ones, when you take upon yourselves those things which I have not asked you to. This night, I ask each of you to come humbly before Me and to repent of your pride, to repent of those times in which you did not listen, those times in which you did not come to ME before you acted. Present all of this to Me and also the hurt that you have sustained because you have been carrying burdens and yokes which are not of Me. My dear ones, when I ask you to carry a burden, I am there to carry it with you. My yoke chafes only when you go from Me and try to do on your own what you decide to do. Come back to Me so that you may be renewed in joy and in peace. I bless you, My dear ones, this night again with My merciful love. Listen to Me.
Notes & Reflections:

JULY 21, 1994
MESSAGE FROM OUR LADY
TO THE WORLD

My dear little children, praise be Jesus! Little children, success in life should not be enmeshed in performance which is only temporary, but should be in God. Do not see God solely as an instrument to your happiness but see Him as the intrinsic way of life. Invest in a success that is of God. Do you not know that all you have has been given to you as a gift from God and not of your own merit? How long will you continue to be complacent with the goodness of God?

Little children, all you do must be done for God, in God and because of God's eternal love for you. All the accomplishments you achieve in your earthly life without Him will only be short-lived because you can do nothing without Him. Only His works are perfect. Seek to please God. He is infinite and you are infinitely important to Him. You have kept your distance from Him and, as a result, are imperfect in love and weak in virtue. If you return to God, He will lovingly mold you in His love, to love and be loved. Place God at the center of your life by surrendering all of your attachments, concerns, fears and manipulating ways to God. Trust in His divine mercy, and love. Interiorly release all your control to God. Be little children dependent totally on God, and be free.

Bless you little ones. I take your petitions to my Son Who is one with the Father. I keep nothing for myself. All is given to Him. Praise be God forever! Peace. Thank you for responding to my call. Ad deum.

Notes & Reflections:

JULY 21, 1994
MESSAGE FROM OUR LORD

My dear ones, I am here again with you this night to speak again plainly to you and not in parables. Each of you is chosen by My Father and so I call you friends. Listen to Me. Know that your Father, My Father, loves you incomparably, unendingly. Know that I love you; that I have given My life for you. I have shown you the way of salvation. My dear ones, you have nothing to fear. You are God's children. I am always with you. Know that My strength is within you. I bless you this night as I remind you that you are never alone. Be encouraged, My dear ones, as you continue your journey. I am with you every step of the way. Peace. I give you this night the blessing of My mercy.

Notes & Reflections:

JULY 28, 1994
MESSAGE FROM OUR LADY

My dear little children, praise be Jesus! Little ones, please love one another with a pure heart. Accept all people in their weakness. Be patient. Love yourself as you are and love others as they are. God loves you as you are. Do not place limitations on your love. Do not restrict your love based off the spirituality of another person. Do not love less because someone does not meet your standards. Love all. Do what is good to others. Only God knows the deepest incentives of the heart. God is infinite. Love unconditionally. Seek to please God and to love as He loves in purity and in fidelity to His goodness. Conversion of heart, sinfulness and uncharitable actions are changed through love and mercy. If you fail, please try again. Great salvation comes to the weak through sincere effort in loving. Even in your sinfulness, as you love and try to live in purity, you do not fail but you are strengthened in humility and in charity.

I bless you little children in the name of my Son and I hear your plea. I take your petitions to my Son's most Sacred Heart. Thank you for responding to my call. Ad deum.

Notes & Reflections:

AUGUST 4, 1994
MESSAGE FROM OUR LADY

My dear little children, praise be Jesus! Little ones, I thank you for your prayers for your country; and I ask you to continue to pray for your country and my beloved Pope. I invite all the little, little children to be consecrated to my Immaculate Heart and to pray every day with their friends and families. There is so much that can be mitigated through prayer. Pray for peace in the world, in your families and in your souls.

My Son has tremendous love for you and does not wish for you to live in turmoil. He desires peace. Peace can exist through prayer and love, but it is necessary that you *respond in action.* Please *respond* by being the fabric of His love. Response to my call of love and mercy through unity, prayer, penance and fasting are important factors can ward off wars and spoken chastisements. I desire to help you, all my children, of this world but you must allow me by *responding* to my Son's plea. He has outlined the path of truth. Give to my son all your pain and all that you hold bound in your heart. Turn to Him. You can be free in God's Love.

I bless you, little ones, and know I am here to bring you hope. Please respond to my call. I take your petitions to my Son's most Sacred Heart. Peace. Ad deum.
Notes & Reflections:

AUGUST 11, 1994
MESSAGE FROM OUR LADY

My dear little children, praise be Jesus! Little children, dedicate yourselves in thankfulness to God. God's peace must be in your hearts. Praise Him with your hearts as well as your lips. I desire you to be close to God, free and happy. I desire for you to live in His joy. Only this can be accomplished through prayer, surrendering to God's direction and giving Him recompense of true sorrow for your sins. Satan is trying to discourage you. He would like you to believe there is no need for penance or faithfulness in fidelity to God. Please, little children, cast off the burden of your sins and allow God to make for you a clean heart and spirit - one of love. My Son does not take pleasure in the death of a soul. He desires all to live in Him. Therefore, little children, over all virtues put on love. Love will bind all other virtues and make them perfect; for God is love and He is perfect for He is Yahweh, your Emmanuel. Bless you, little ones, in the name of Jesus. I take your petitions to Him Who has allowed me to be here with you. Thank you for responding to my call. Peace. Ad deum.
Notes & Reflections:

AUGUST 11, 1994
MESSAGE FROM OUR LORD

My dear ones, I come to you this night to remind you again of My presence here with you; to remind you again of My presence within your hearts; to remind you again that I am with you always. I know, My dear ones, that as you look upon this world the power of evil is so overwhelming. You are forgetting that I have overcome this world. Your heads are so turned with spectacular events. My dear ones, I am here to remind you what is of importance is never seen by the human eye. It is the miracle of change and conversion that is worked within your heart, if you allow Me to be there with you. As you allow that conversion, you will not not be so overwhelmed and over-awed by spectacular happenings. You will know the truth and so you will be truly free. This night I tell you that the road to true freedom within Me is forgiveness. It is the key to the Kingdom of God, and so this night, My dear ones, I, Who have paid the price of your redemption with My very blood, bless you with strength to forgive. Accept My blessing and live in the freedom of God.

Notes & Reflections:

AUGUST 18, 1994
MESSAGE FROM OUR LADY

My dear children, praise be Jesus! Little children, take the time to enjoy and appreciate with gratitude all the gifts and blessings my Son has granted and betrothed unto you. Believe with all your heart in your salvation and immerse yourself in His love. God loves you, little ones. Live in total confidence of His love, knowing he will take care of you. He will not forsake you, for you have been called by name. Love one another. Have no fear. Trust in God. Be dependent on God's love as little children. Please do not form negative opinions or pass judgment on one another. Be aware of your own actions and love unconditionally.

Focus on God and your own relationship with Him. Strive to serve Him in humility. You cannot serve God when love is lacking. If you harbor emotions of bitterness, anger, jealousy, hatred or *complacency* toward one another you are unable to serve God in humility. To serve God there must be love, for God is love.

I bless you, little children, in the name of Jesus and I thank you for responding to my call. Ad deum.

Notes & Reflections:

NOTES & REFLECTIONS:

NOTES & REFLECTIONS:

NOTES & REFLECTIONS:

NOTES & REFLECTIONS:

NOTES & REFLECTIONS:

NOTES & REFLECTIONS: